10J

THE
INSPIRED
GARDEN

THE
INSPIRED
GARDEN

IMAGINATIVE
IDEAS AND FEATURES
IN FULL COLOUR

DEREK FELL

HEADLINE

A FRIEDMAN GROUP BOOK

Copyright ©1987 by Michael Friedman Publishing Group, Inc.

First published in Great Britain in 1987 by
HEADLINE BOOK PUBLISHING PLC

HEADLINE BOOK PUBLISHING PLC
Headline House
79 Great Titchfield Street
London W1P 7FN

British Library Cataloguing in Publication Data
Fell, Derek
The Inspired Garden
1. Landscape gardening—Amateurs'
manuals   I. Title
712' .6 SB473

ISBN 0-7472-0029-7

THE INSPIRED GARDEN:
Imaginative Ideas and Features in Full Colour
was prepared and produced by
Michael Friedman Publishing Group, Inc.
15 West 26th Street
New York, N.Y. 10010

Editors: Louise Quayle/Nancy Kalish
Art Director: Mary Moriarty
Designer: Liz Trovato
Photo Editor: Philip Hawthorne
Production Manager: Karen L. Greenberg

Typeset by BPE Graphics, Inc.
Colour separations by Hong Kong Scanner Craft Company Ltd.
Printed and bound in Hong Kong by Leefung-Asco Printers Ltd.

DEDICATION

For my three children: Tina, Derek Jr., and Victoria

ACKNOWLEDGMENTS

Special thanks to Hiroshi Makita, garden designer,
who helped me understand the Oriental philosophy of landscape design
as expressed in this book.

Also to Elizabeth A. Murray, garden designer—
the only woman and only American to have worked in Claude Monet's garden
at Giverny, France—who helped me understand the influence of
Monet's garden on today's garden designs.

And to the late Harry Smith, English gentleman,
who taught me how to photograph gardens.

CONTENTS

INTRODUCTION

The best gardens are much more than an assortment of beautiful plants. Successful gardens generally represent a careful integration of diverse elements, ranging from the purely ornamental to the strictly functional. Paths, pools, planters, trellises, arbours, fountains, and fences can contribute enormously to the creation of an exciting and harmonious garden. The same attention one brings to decorating a house and making it "livable" can be used to make a garden a pleasant place to find privacy, to meditate, and to escape the pressures of a fast-moving, machine-oriented world.

It's a fact that man-made garden features establish the "style" of a garden more definitively than plants alone. Period gardens—Victorian, French, Renaissance, Elizabethan, Japanese Imperial—all demand the proper placement of structural and design elements to make them recognizable. Indeed, the simple addition of a particular style of gazebo, bench, or arbour can instantly "identify" a garden. Similarly, with "ethnic" gardens—such as an English cottage garden, a Chinese meditation garden, or an Italian water garden—the selection of appropriate fences, bridges, and ornaments brings style and a sense of permanence to the environment.

The world over, there are structures that "make" a garden's reputation. At Magnolia Gardens, near Charleston, South Carolina (U.S.A.), for example, a sleek trellised footbridge called The Long Bridge is a "trademark" of the garden. Its distinctive design, traversing the corner of a cypress lake, is immediately identifiable. Somewhat French in style, painted white to contrast with the dark water and the tall cypress trees draped with Spanish moss, the bridge helps create a romantic atmosphere, which probably makes it the subject of more photographs and paintings than any other garden structure in the world.

Though some structures look good unadorned, as part of a garden composition, others are enhanced by some kind of plant decoration. British gardeners are especially fond of training climbing roses, wisteria, honeysuckle, and ivy up walls, fences, gazebos, and summerhouses, sometimes so successfully that the structure becomes completely covered in vines, flowers, or foliage.

Then there are features that rely on plants alone for dramatic impact. At Levens Hall in the English Lake District, towering chess pieces of clipped English yew provide such a whimsical highlight that the topiary figures have made the garden world famous. Some of the specimens are so massive they have rooms inside them, entered through archways. In North America this kind of clever topiary work inspired the famous Ladew Topiary Gardens, near Baltimore, Maryland, where there is a foxhunting scene of clipped Japanese yew—a horse and rider chasing five hounds and a fox across a front lawn.

The roles of plantsman and architect in the creation of a beautiful garden are important, but their efforts may fall short without a third important influence—the contribution of artist. The best gardens today seem to combine the talents of plantsman, architect, and artist. Sometimes these three skills are embodied in a single person (Major Lawrence Johnston, owner of Hidcote Garden and Vita Sackville-West, owner of Sissinghurst Garden—two outstanding English gardens—come immediately to mind); but more frequently they are achieved by a pooling of talents. For example, the beautiful American estate garden of Filoli, near San Francisco, is a result of the collaboration of Isabella Worn, a plantsperson, and Bruce Porter, a landscape painter. Porter did the overall arrangement of spaces and features, and Worn developed the planting schemes and selected the plants.

Impressionist painter Claude Monet was an artist who embodied skills as a plantsman and architect in designing his garden at Giverny, in France. Monet created very simple but stunning flower beds for the entrance of his house. To complement his pink stucco house with distinctive green shutters he planted solid blocks of pink geraniums studded with pink and white rose standards. He bordered these raised flower beds with grey foliaged dianthus. Bold blocks of colour, carefully selected to blend with the nearby structure, is the key to success of this particular garden space.

Gardens can also be repositories for works of art. These artworks need not be realistic to be an effective embellishment. Garden art began as symbolism in rocks and dead wood, the ancient Chinese bringing into their gardens boulders representing images of mammals. They gave these rock formations names such as "turtle rock," "owl rock," and "dragon rock" for the objects they resembled. From symbolism in rocks and dead wood, garden makers became obsessed with realism. The more anatomically correct a sculpture, the more highly valued it became, reaching its height in Ancient Greece and Italy with statues of gods and heroes placed on pedestals in garden settings.

Today the art world has turned full circle, with an emphasis once again on symbolism and impressionism. Indeed, artist Esteban Vicente put it well when asked to explain an apparent paradox between the modernistic style of his art and his love of gardening as a hobby. "You cannot make art if you are not involved with nature," he said. "Anything to do with nature has to do with art."

The Long Bridge at Magnolia Plantation, in South Carolina, (U.S.A.), is such a classic feature it has become a trademark of American Southern-style gardens.

Previous page: A horse and rider, clipped out of Japanese yew, chase hounds and fox at the Ladew Topiary Garden, in Maryland (U.S.A.). This scene was inspired by a less elaborate design the owner saw in England.

CHAPTER ONE

CONCEPTS
AND STYLES

An Italian-style terrace at Hearst Castle, in California (U.S.A.), contrasts terra-cotta tiles with white marble, using an ornate marble font as a decorative highlight. The expansive terrace overlooks a spectacular vista of hills sweeping down to the Pacific Ocean.

The origin of gardens is not clear cut. There are historians who say the first gardens were food gardens, which must have developed soon after the process of germination was discovered in seeds. This led to the production of fruit crops, such as melons and later, cereal grains. In Egyptian tombs, ancient wall paintings provide evidence of garden spaces 5,000 years ago planted with citrus and figs. The development of gardens using ornamental plants for purely decorative effect came much later, possibly not until the Roman and Chinese cultures were well established roughly 2,500 years ago. However, even before humans learned to plant seeds for food they looked upon a green environment as a safe haven—particularly a grassland and tree-rich environment presenting long vistas for the detection of prey and predators. Green plants became associated with comfort—a source of shelter and the presence of food and water.

Pliny the Younger (A.D. 62–113), a Roman statesman and philosopher, wrote many letters describing his villas and gardens. He makes the first reference to *topiary,* which is the art of pruning trees and shrubs into shapes. "You descend to a sloping garden through an avenue of box cut, topiary fashion, into the shapes of animals..." he wrote to a friend, and ever since this garden has been referred to in horticultural literature as "Pliny's Topiary Zoo."

This French Renaissance-style garden has a vista leading to a temple of love as its focal point. The flat terrain and openness of the design, plus Versailles-style trees in containers, parterre hedges, and gravel walks are typical of French château gardens.

"Organized chaos" is a term appropriate to this English-style perennial garden. The exuberant colour of the hardy plants is contained by a barn wall. A white trellis adds a good vertical feature as well as support for climbing roses.

Jasmine Hill, in Alabama (U.S.A.), features Greek statuary reminiscent, in its emphasis on realism in art, of ancient Rome. Ferns and succulents in tubs and urns on flagstone complement the statuary, while ornamental trees and shrubs form a pleasant background.

THE ORIENTAL INFLUENCE

At the other end of the world, isolated from European influence until Marco Polo's penetration through the vast mountain ranges and desolate deserts filled with savage tribes, the Chinese developed another art form involving trees. They were the first to use *bonsai* in their gardens, by transplanting miniature trees found growing in the wild, dwarfed by wind, salt spray, or rocky soil. However, it was the Japanese who then created bonsai artificially, by selective pruning of branches and restricting the roots in shallow containers.

The Oriental garden was the first to become a living, artistic structure—an attempt to humanize nature's wildness. Materials of lasting value (particularly wood, stone, gravel, and sand) were introduced. An early form of Oriental garden was the *cup garden*. This could be large enough to encompass a lake surrounded by hills—the lake surface forming the bottom of the cup and the slopes of the hills its sides—with walking trails leading to smaller cup gardens in the hillsides. Or on the smallest scale, a cup garden could be nothing more than a stone slab with a bonsai in the middle. The purpose of a cup garden was introspection and privacy, using definite focal points and symbolism for a close communication with nature. Makers of cup gardens studied the natural order of things— the many ways water can fall into a pool, the contours of hills, the sinuous lines of trees sculpted by a harsh environment— and they sought to symbolize these powerful images in their intimate gardens.

In particular, the concept of a cup garden includes drawing the viewer's attention to something special. It might be a plant, a boulder, a pond, or even a building. The ancient Chinese were fond of surrounding themselves with enclosures to shut out the chaos and clutter of civilization. They built earthen mounds, elaborate walls, hedges, and fences to provide isolation, creating within these structures their own small realm of beauty. However, it was not a static environment. The Chinese deliberately designed their gardens for strolling. They liked to walk leisurely along serpentine paths that made maximum use of the terrain, with surprises—or "pictures"—at every turn, something new always coming into view. Plants were only one element used in creating these pictures. Rocks, waterfalls, viewing platforms, bridges, overlooks, and shelters became important components of a garden, making the stroll an adventure. Indeed, the placement of a structure was more important than the structure itself. The

This Japanese garden of Swiss pines was inspired by the Imperial Gardens of Kyoto, Japan, which took their inspiration from ancient Chinese garden art and philosophy.

gardens between strong and subtle features.

The poet-painter Wang Wei (A.D. 699–759), of the T'ang Dynasty, is believed to have created the first cup garden, in the rugged hills in Shensi, where he built for his mother a garden called Wang Ch'uan. Our knowledge of this early garden comes from a scroll painting by Wang Wei himself. Though the original has been lost, there are copies of it showing gardens with buildings and pavilions placed in a rugged landscape close to a river. A trail winds among hills and forest clearings from one garden space to another. Many of the gardens are enclosed by a bamboo thicket, a stone wall, or a picket fence. Some contain orchard trees, while others appear to be designed as secret places for study and contemplation.

The early Chinese cup gardens strongly influenced the Japanese, and many examples of these Chinese origins can be seen today in the three imperial gardens in the ancient Japanese capital of Kyoto. They are the Sento Imperial Palace Garden, the Garden at Katsura Detached Palace, and the Garden of the Shungaku-in Detached Palace. Created more than three centuries ago, these magnificent gardens probably have had more influence on Japanese garden design—both in Japan and around the world—than any other Japanese gardens. Commonly called *stroll gardens,* for the paths that wander through them, the three gardens are famous for a number of special features: a stone promontory at Katsura, a beach of egg-shaped stones at Sento, and powerful stonework at Shugaku-in. These features have inspired imitation and adaptation throughout the world.

Perhaps the finest example of a Chinese cup garden outside China can be seen today at the estate called Innisfree, near Millbrook, New York (U.S.A.). Created by Walter Beck, a painter, and his wife, Marion, whose wealth was derived from iron ore deposits in the Midwest, the garden lies 70 miles (113 kilometers) north of New York City in a magnificent rugged landscape. Though Beck never visited China, he was inspired by historical documents and paintings; at his country home he surrounded a beautiful cobalt-blue lake with his interpretation of a Chinese cup garden.

Landscape architect Lester Collins, who knew Walter Beck well, remembers Beck saying that the Chinese did not look *at* a picture, they looked *into* it. To enter Innisfree, with its labyrinth of winding paths and fantastic stonework, is akin to taking a stroll and entering a garden picture, says Collins. Beck worked energetically on expanding the garden right up to his death at age ninety-one. He declared that making a garden was one of the finest forms of art, ranking with the arts of music and painting. Innisfree—which is now open to the public—still lives up to that claim.

buildings in a classic Chinese garden are first and foremost garden features, just as the hills, rocks, streams, ponds, trees, and flowers are garden features.

The philosophy of the ancient Chinese was to seek a union between man and nature. They regarded the rivers as arteries, the mountains as the bones of a skeleton, and garden makers searched the natural world for system and order. To help make sense of the nature, the Chinese adopted the principles of *yin* (female) and *yang* (male). The yin-yang philosophy identified placid water as "yin" and protruding boulders as "yang," for example. An understanding of this philosophy helped early Chinese garden designers strike a balance in their

THE EUROPEAN INFLUENCE

This terrace at Jasmine Hill Garden, in Alabama (U.S.A.), features Southern-style wrought-iron railings and trelliswork, helping to frame a beautiful view.

This small, American Colonial-style garden makes good use of evergreens, including English boxwood and English ivy, to make a pleasant garden room.

The antithesis of the Chinese cup garden and the Japanese stroll garden is the extravagant garden style that began in Italy during the Renaissance, and which was then taken to even grander heights in France. These elaborate gardens sought to stun the senses with magnificent vistas, architectural splendour, and spaciousness. The passion for unrestricted views, parklike landscapes, and sculptural grandeur even crossed the Channel to England. Eventually the English rebelled and produced a new style of landscape design, with an emphasis on informality—a type of organized chaos, featuring companion plantings with an emphasis on colour combinations, foliage, texture, and plant form.

By the mid-fifteenth century, the Renaissance was reaching its peak in Italy. Trade with other countries was flourishing and produced extraordinary wealth for the merchants, the religious hierarchy, and the noble classes of society. The combination of wealth and contact with other nations stimulated a high level of appreciation in the arts and sciences, and some of the world's most fantastic gardens were completed during this period. Today the word *Italianate*—when applied to a garden—evokes images of grandeur accented by elaborate parterres, gushing fountains, baroque sculptures, fern-filled grottoes, massive stone terraces, steeply descending steps, balustrades, vine-clad arbours, marble temples, spacious plazas, and splendid urns. But most of all, the term Italianate means spectacular vistas and avenues of towering, precisely spaced cypress trees leading the eye towards breathtaking views of spectacular scenery.

The garden that has influenced more Italianate gardens around the world than any other is the Villa d'Este, at Tivoli, near Rome. Although this garden was inspired by earlier Italian gardens—notably the Villa Lante, north of Rome—the Villa d'Este is to Italy what the gardens of Versailles are to France: a marvel of landscape design that positively shocks the senses.

Built for the governor of Tivoli, Cardinal Ippolito d'Este II, by architect Pirro Ligorio, around 1550, the Villa d'Este is situated on an extremely steep hillside with tremendous flights of steps accentuating a main axis down the slope to give the illusion of even greater distance. Terraces form cross-axes, with fountains and plazas, balustrades and arches, as architectural highlights so that the view up the slope is as astonish-

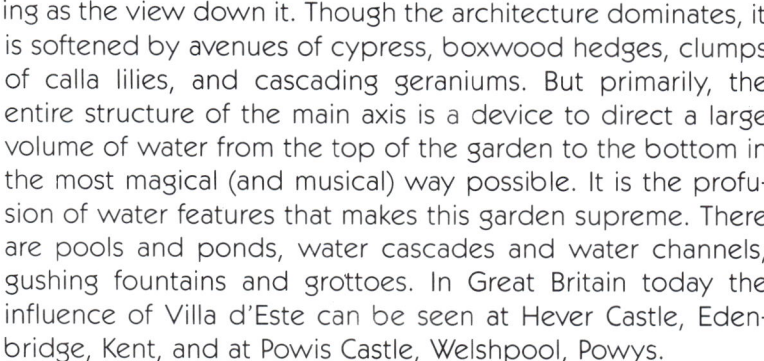

A gazebo and footbridge, together with splashes of colour from old-fashioned flowering annuals, help to create a romantic Victorian garden.

This English-style cottage garden places typical British emphasis on plants as features.

ing as the view down it. Though the architecture dominates, it is softened by avenues of cypress, boxwood hedges, clumps of calla lilies, and cascading geraniums. But primarily, the entire structure of the main axis is a device to direct a large volume of water from the top of the garden to the bottom in the most magical (and musical) way possible. It is the profusion of water features that makes this garden supreme. There are pools and ponds, water cascades and water channels, gushing fountains and grottoes. In Great Britain today the influence of Villa d'Este can be seen at Hever Castle, Edenbridge, Kent, and at Powis Castle, Welshpool, Powys.

The Renaissance spread from Italy to France in the sixteenth century, and during the seventeenth century French statesmen and nobility built extravagant gardens, taking inspiration from the gardens of Italy and even persuading Italian artisans to help them. However, there were important differences. For one thing, the land around Paris was largely flat, whereas near Rome the Italians had steep hillsides to build on. To compensate for the lack of elevation and still overshadow the Italians, the French began to make gardens with excessively wide avenues and vistas so long they disappeared over the horizon. They made everything geometric and expansive in scale—oval reflecting pools of an acre or more, rectangular

canals big enough for a fleet of rowing boats, and parterres larger than a football field, with plantings in scroll patterns and flourishes far more elaborate than anything seen in Italy. Nicholas Fouquet, minister of finance to Louis XIV, created such an extravagant formal garden at Vaux-le-Vicomte that he angered the king, and soon after opening the estate with a series of fêtes, Fouquet was dismissed from his position and thrown into jail—where he remained until his death nineteen years later.

The envious King Louis commanded Fouquet's architect, interior designer, and landscape architect to eclipse their previous works with the creation of the world's most grandiose structure—the Palace of Versailles.

Out of a marsh, landscape architect André Le Nôtre made a garden of such spaciousness that it virtually has no equal. Every structure and garden feature seems larger than life— incredibly wide allées, elaborate fountains, massive reflecting pools, folly gardens, sunken gardens, rock gardens, and many other treasures tucked away in odd corners beyond the central formality. There is an entire complex of quaint thatched cottages surrounding a water-lily pond, as well as a "mountain" landscape of boulders and cliffs with caves, trails, and secret passages where courtiers played hide-and-seek.

Such was the impact of this creation that in the 1920s, when American industrialists and entrepreneurs began to make fortunes from railroads, shipping, mining, and manufacturing, it became fashionable to emulate Versailles. All across America—at Newport, Rhode Island, on the south shore of Long Island, in southern California, and around Philadelphia—wealthy Americans attempted to reproduce its splendor. Though many of these examples have since fallen into ruin through lack of enthusiasm—or lack of funds—to maintain them, some of the best still remain and are open to the public: Nemours, near Wilmington, Delaware, the former home of Alfred I. duPont; and Biltmore House and Garden, near Ashville, North Carolina, an estate that has a vista offering a 30-mile view (50 kilometers) into the Blue Ridge Mountains.

Versailles influenced the design of Hampton Court's gardens, near London, when King Charles II remodelled the palace in the 1600s. The splendid Versailles-style allées—set out in the pattern of a goose foot—are still seen today. In later years, however, the British rebelled against formality in gardens and developed a new style of gardening referred to as *naturalism,* which is in fact a misnomer, since the best examples all have a strong design sense. However, instead of plants being "bedded-out" in squares and rectangles in the French style, the British used them informally, mixing heights, colours, and textures, allowing vines to sprawl up and over a wall, filling cracks in paving with alpine plants, establishing dry walls with succulents cascading from them, crowding beds and borders and urns to overflowing. British garden designers and writers William Robinson and Gertrude Jekyll helped popularize naturalism. "Planned disorder" is a phrase that accurately describes this approach. It's a style of gardening that places a much greater emphasis on plants than on architecture, and it gave rise to the popularity of perennials and flowering shrubs for achieving the effect. Metaphorically, the plants become colours in an artist's palette, and they are applied to the landscape in broad sweeps and delicate dabs, as an impressionist artist would daub paint on a canvas. Colour gardens also became the vogue, as exemplified by the white garden at Sissinghurst, the blue garden at Hever Castle, the red garden at Hidcote, and other gardens of green and yellow.

In addition to colour themes, the British developed gardens featuring a particular genus, or plant family. This grew out of their interest in plant collecting as the British Empire expanded and brought discoveries of exotic plant populations in South Africa, Australia, and North America in particular. First came fern gardens and rose gardens, followed by heather gardens, rhododendron gardens, peony gardens, and lilac gardens. Another type of British theme garden takes advantage of a geological feature to create a stage for presenting plants that are often referred to as "players." A bog garden was a stage for introducing the charms of primulas, iris, and other plants that like wet feet. After British exploration of the Alps and the Himalayas, with particularly rich finds of new plant material, rock gardens caught on as a theme, mixing heaths and heathers with ferns, succulents, and alpine plants.

At Giverny, in France, impressionist painter Claude Monet took inspiration from cottage gardens he saw in Normandy and created a magnificent garden with a painterly eye towards dramatic colour combinations. In addition to masses of flowering plants he used structures as garden features to add

The Biltmore House and Garden, in North Carolina (U.S.A.), took its inspiration from Versailles Palace, in France. Here, a sculpture of Diane, the huntress, and her hound provides a focal point along a vista facing the main house.

dimension to his garden—high arched trellises for climbing roses to create a ''grande allée'' leading to his front door, a Japanese-style footbridge spanning a water-lily pond (the bridge itself covered with a canopy of wisteria), and stylish benches for admiring the beauty of his garden. Today, the restored garden of Monet is itself inspiring more new garden design throughout the world than any other garden.

It is clear from these examples of inspired gardens that certain features—both natural and artificial—are needed to create a spectacular garden. *The Inspired Garden* looks at the most important elements that make designing a garden of accents a successful endeavor.

The gardens of Hearst Castle, located in California (U.S.A.), high on a mountaintop overlooking the Pacific Ocean, are Italianate in design and emulate gardens such as the Villa d'Este near Rome.

CHAPTER TWO

PAVING, DECKS, WALKS, AND STEPS

A simple Oriental-style wooden deck provides a good view of a backyard garden.

Paths, steps, and terraces are used to guide a person through a garden—moving here, pausing there. An important element in the functioning of a garden, they can also be accents of great beauty.

The kind of path you construct should depend on the sense of movement you want to create. Straight and narrow paths tend to quicken the pace and keep the walker's vision fixed at the horizon; broad, meandering paths encourage slower movement, allowing visitors to walk abreast, look up and above, and converse in a leisuredly manner. Stepping stones slow the pace drastically as a concentrated effort is needed to negotiate them. They force us to look at the ground

These steps of rough stone, covered with fallen leaves, embellish a slope in an Oriental garden. Note how the grass-like liriope, ivy, low azalea bushes, and golden euonymus complement the dark, stark beauty of the rocks. Also note how the steps stop short of the crest of the slope and allow a pathway to complete the change in elevation.

and in particular at the destination they lead to. Narrow steps are difficult to negotiate and slow us down; wide steps speed us along, tempting us to go up or down them at a fast clip.

Porches and terraces are popular gathering places, though porches tend to be more a part of the house than of the garden, and are generally screened to keep away insects. Many porches are enclosed, with sliding glass doors to give protection from weather.

Terraces to be used for socializing should be easily accessible from the house. If contiguous with a room of the house, such as a living room or dining room, it is important to provide a step down to the terrace in order to weatherproof the living area. In deciding between the installation of a terrace and a deck, cost becomes a factor. On steep gradients where the footings are some distance below, it becomes easier and less expensive to build a deck.

A main terrace should be paved with a durable, solid, all-weather surface. It should be level and free of cracks or ill-fitting joints. Flagstone is a popular paving material for terraces, and there is a great temptation to space the joints wide enough to grow moss, thyme, or tiny clumps of sedum between them. However, this can make movement difficult. An intelligent compromise is to make one area of terrace as firm and smooth as possible for sitting and standing—such as a semicircle or a square—and let the area beyond it have a more rugged appearance.

Both flagstone and brick can be laid dry on sand or clinker (to form a drainage medium), but greater stability is assured with a concrete foundation.

A popular material for decks is pressure-treated pine, using two-by-fours nailed onto floor joists with about a half-inch separation to allow water to drain away. Before constructing a deck, consider whether you want it covered to keep out rain or uncovered to give an unobstructed view. A good compromise might be to keep half the deck covered and leave half of it uncovered so you can enjoy the best of both worlds.

Of course, all paved areas should be scaled to fit in with other elements of the garden, but in designing paved areas there is a tendency to make them too small. Allowance should be made for the encroachment of plants if beds and borders edge a paved area, and in the case of paths sufficient "elbow room" is necessary so that visitors do not feel they are treading a tightrope. A width of at least 4 feet (1.25 meters) is recommended for the narrowest path. Where paths are bordered by hedges, provision should be made for the natural spread of the plants.

Old brick helps to create a cartwheel design and comfortable walking surface in this garden room where beds of impatiens surround a water-lily pool.

A boardwalk is used to provide passage through a boggy area, with a small humpback footbridge to traverse a narrow stream.

CHOOSING A SURFACE

The primary purpose of any paving is to provide comfort for the feet, and especially to keep feet dry. Paving should produce a firm non-skid surface. A hard surface—such as flagstone—is more comfortable for feet that must remain still for a long time. Therefore, places for socializing, eating, resting, and admiring a view tend to favour hard, solid materials such as brick and flagstone. Paths, on the other hand, can use softer materials, to cushion the feet and reduce noise.

Brick, stone, tile, gravel, sand, concrete, and wood are popular materials for paths and steps. For paths, shredded leaves, shredded pine bark, ground limestone, crushed seashells, wood chips, pine needles, and other organic products are also good choices. They facilitate drainage and add a distinctive touch to the look of the garden.

Prime importance should be given to drainage. "Puddling" is a common problem on terraces and paths. Where drainage is a problem, paths can be made with a camber, or curvature, to direct rainfall into channels. Loose path surfaces may have a tendency to flush away after heavy rains. Lightweight organic materials such as pine needles may need constant replenishment in exposed areas and are better suited to protected situations.

How a surface will look after rainfall is a very important consideration. For example, certain kinds of flagstone can produce a beautiful reflection and "shine" even after a light shower, considerably enhancing the garden's visual appeal. Similarly, pine needles in a woodland setting will turn a distinctive chestnut brown after rain and will infuse the atmosphere with a delicate pine fragrance.

Where snow accumulation can be expected, consider surfaces that will make its disposal easy. On smooth surfaces, such as flagstone, snow is easily removed, but on gravel or pebble surfaces it is difficult; with every shovelful of snow you'll scoop up precious quantities of stone.

In choosing paving material, also consider the character of the garden. For example, in gardens close to the shore, crushed oyster shels, white landscape chips, and pine needles are extremely attractive. Gravel is popular for formal areas, and brick is desirable for Tudor-style gardens.

PAVING MATERIALS

Bricks can be purchased new or used, the used kind generally costing more and adding a sense of maturity. A great many patterns can be made with bricks, and they can be laid to form a square, rectangle, diamond shape, oval, or circle. Bricks make an excellent surface for paths as well as for gathering places, though it is advisable to have a container of sand nearby to sprinkle on them to prevent slipping during wet or icy weather. Good examples of brick paving are found in the garden at Hidcote, near Chipping Campden, Gloucestershire, and at Barrington Court, near Ilminster, Somerset.

Concrete is an inexpensive paving material and quite versatile. Commonly, concrete is laid in round or square slabs, shaped by forms. It can be textured with a wire brush or coloured with powders to make it look less utilitarian. At Jasmine Hill, a beautiful sculpture garden near Montgomery, Alabama (U.S.A.), the owners made concrete paths more aesthetically pleasing by pressing large tropical leaves into wet concrete squares to make a decorative imprint. Seashells, pebbles, and tiles are also popular embellishments to a concrete surface.

Flagstone is a wonderful paving material, whether used in squares and rectangles, circles, or "crazy paving" with sharp edges and varied shapes. When buying flagstone check with a local quarry to see if an indigenous stone is available. Unusual colours and textures unique to a particular area of the country can help to produce a harmonious effect.

It's important to decide how far apart to set the joints. The flags can be butted together so closely you can hardly pass a razor blade between them, or set sufficiently far apart to allow mosses, sedums, and alpine plants to grow. Flagstone establishes an incredibly good feeling of stability and longevity. Consider it *first* among paving materials, but keep in mind that, like brick, flagstone gets slippery in wet or icy weather and must be sanded.

Wood has the advantage of being easy to work with and relatively inexpensive. It is best used in situations where a flat deck or boardwalk is needed over difficult terrain. Landscape ties and railroad ties can be used alone or in combination with stones and gravel to make decks and paths, the ties forming a frame. Wood "rounds" simulating sliced slabs of a tree trunk make good stepping stones, especially when sunk into gravel or concrete.

Wood chips, pine bark, garden peat, and pine needles are examples of organic materials popular for surfacing paths. Wood chips are readily available from neighborhood work crews and are the least expensive, though pine bark, garden peat, and pine needles tend to be more attractive.

Informal steps using stone risers and wide gravel treads allow rock plants to spill into this pathway.

Broken flagstone makes a perfect surface for this shaded patio garden that uses a number of prominent garden features, including statuary, an arbour, and plants in containers. The flagstone area is sufficiently large to accommodate a substantial group of people either seated or standing.

A flagstone path, edged with hostas and shaded by deciduous trees, runs along the edge of a lawn and leads to a garden seat.

STEPS AND STEPPING-STONES

Whenever a change of elevation is needed, steps become important. For only a slight change, a single stone step, with a gently rising path beyond, may be all that's necessary to negotiate a slope. However, for steeper inclines all manner of formal and informal steps can be used.

Steps are composed of two basic parts—there is the *tread* (which is the flat part on which people walk) and the *riser* (the vertical part between treads). It is the size and shape of the tread, plus the height and style of the riser, which allow so many variations in design for steps. For example, treads can be made from overlapping millstones, and from bricks, railroad ties, and wooden slabs. Risers can be of the same material or of a different material, but the risers should be more or less uniform. The width of the tread and the height of the riser dictates movement. For example, low risers and wide treads encourage faster steps than narrow treads with high risers. People tend to take a straight flight of steps a good deal faster than a curving flight, and if an ascent is unusually long, then a recess can be made to fit a bench for allowing visitors to catch their breath. Handrails are another possible design feature. For steep slopes they are a safety feature, but in many situations a rail can be considered for purely ornamental effect.

A good sense of scale is essential when planning steps. For a short climb narrow steps might work well, but for long distances wider treads are usually more comfortable and aesthetically pleasing.

It's useful to know that for an indoor setting, architects use a strict formula for designing steps—usually stipulating treads that are 30.5 centimeters wide and with risers 15 centimeters high. For indoor living, this uniformity is important for the sake of comfort and safety. However, in an outdoor environment people do not expect such uniformity and have the time to adjust their pace to negotiate different types of steps. Even so, experience shows that risers less than 10 centimeters or more than 18 centimeters high become irritating or difficult to climb, and though treads can extend to any width beyond 122 centimeters, the ideal depth is 28 to 35.5 centimeters.
Steps can climb in a direct, straight line, or they can reach their destination in a gentle curve or zigzag. In most situations brick, stone, and wood—particularly landscape ties—are good materials to consider. However, grass can be a particularly pleasing surface for steps in areas that are not heavily

trampled. Lawn grass is restful on the eye, comfortable on the feet, and works particularly well where a slope is gradual, and where treads can be sufficiently wide and deep to accommodate a lawn mower or lawn trimmer.

Steps should harmonize with their surroundings. Obviously, steps made from rough fieldstone—well suited to an Oriental or English cottage garden—may be out of place in a highly formal French Renaissance garden.

Good materials to consider as stepping-stones are millstones (with the center hole filled in with cement) and level fieldstones. Concrete can be used to simulate millstones if the real thing proves difficult to obtain. Also, concrete can be used to create different shapes of stepping stones. Square slabs laid out in a symmetrical or random design can be particularly effective.

In gardens with low-lying areas—such as bog gardens—stepping-stones should be used only for short distances. Where a large expanse of wet ground has to be negotiated, it may be better to construct a boardwalk, since the novelty of stepping stones soon becomes tiresome for most people, and even dangerous.

This brick walkway at Filoli Garden, near San Francisco (U.S.A.), ascends a slope by means of short flights of steps. Note how the varying widths of treads and the narrow risers have been used to produce a distinctive design.

Facing page: Cement paving, enhanced with pebbles, provides an attractive, firm surface for walking, to which cascading cotoneaster is a beautiful contrast.

A rugged flight of sandstone steps, making use of beach boulders, leads from a secluded cove up a steep cliff to a seaside cottage garden.

DRIVEWAYS AND PARKING AREAS

There is a notion among landscape architects that the best kind of parking area for cars is a wide circular driveway of Belgian blocks at the front entrance to the house, with a high brick wall festooned with climbing hydrangeas surrounding the parking area to screen it from adjacent areas of the garden. Alternatively, one might consider a quarter-mile-long cobblestone or tarmac driveway that gently sweeps uphill through a grove of tall evergreen trees, with automatic wrought-iron gates at the street, which open and close at the touch of a button from inside the owner's car. Unfortunately, very few of us have the means or the space to indulge in this kind of luxury.

For many homeowners the only parking space available is the street itself, or a short driveway into a one-car garage attached to the house, or, worse, a detached garage at the rear of the property reached by a narrow gravel driveway. Too often, in even the best-designed modern houses, the driveway and parking area is too conspicuous, too garish with its utilitarian coating of black asphalt. Interestingly, studies have shown that landscaping a parking area and driveway is one of the top projects undertaken by new home owners.

First, which paving material is the most suitable should be considered—brick or Belgian blocks are obviously good choices in areas with snow cover in winter, as snow removal is easy. Next, consider a low hedge to line the driveway—one sufficiently high to screen the drive but not high enough to restrict vision. Instead of a continuous hedge, you might prefer a line of closely spaced pollution-resistant yew or holly, forming cushions or cones.

Consider these suggestions for turning driveways into attractive features:

1. Consider erecting a carport over part of the driveway and planting flowering vines to create a canopy of flowers and foliage.

2. Extend a deck from the house over part of the driveway and assemble a collection of planters on the deck—including some window-box planters—so foliage and flowers can cascade from the deck for decorative effect.

3. Line the driveway with estate planters filled with trees and shrubs. Estate planters are generally made of wood, painted white, and simulate a style of container used at Versailles, in France. Other ornate containers for trees and shrubs include half-barrels, terra-cotta tubs and ornate urns.

4. Make a double flower border filled with flowering annuals or perennials so a twin ribbon of colour flanks the driveway all the way up to the garage door.

5. Line one or both sides of the driveway with statues set on pedestals.

6. If the driveway features a turn-around circle, consider placing a fountain in the middle of the circle, or a colourful circular flower bed.

7. Arch the driveway over with rustic or metal arches for climbing roses, and other flowering vines, to scramble over.

Top: *Concrete edging bordering a driveway helps to protect a clump of oaks against accidental damage by cars.*

Bottom: *This formal entrance to an estate provides both a strong sense of security and a sense of welcome to invited guests.*

Facing page: *Broken flagstone, also known as "crazy paving," creates a firm surface. Gaps between stones have been spaced deliberately wide so that clumps of cushion pinks, moss, and thyme can be planted to soften the lines in future years.*

CHAPTER THREE

LAWNS, MOSS, AND GROUNDCOVER PLANTS

This garden demonstrates a happy marriage between the informality of native trees and the geometry of a formal lawn and pool feature.

There may be less labour-intensive ways to cover large expanses of bare ground than installing a lawn—including the use of concrete, flagstone, and evergreen ground-hugging plants—but nothing is quite so restful to look at, so comfortable to walk on, so soft and safe for playing, lounging, or picnicking, as a grass lawn.

Lawns have a soothing influence in gardens. They simulate clearings in a forest or evoke visions of verdant meadows that have been closely cropped by woolly sheep. Besides its velvety appearance, hard-wearing quality, softness, and smooth contour, a grass lawn stabilizes dust, provides erosion control, has a cooling effect on the environment, reduces noise and glare, refreshes the atmosphere, and has the ability to add substantially to the cash value of a residential property.

Shadows can play an important part in the visual pleasure of a lawn. At noon many lawns can look plain, but as the sun dips in the sky, shadows from surrounding trees and structures can pencil a tapestry of patterns across the greensward.

The grading of a lawn can produce equally dramatic effects, especially if it contains gentle curves, pitches, and dips. At Middleton Place plantation, in South Carolina (U.S.A.), there is a magnificent lawn descending a slope in a series of terraces, producing long shadows in the early morning and late afternoon. At Dumbarton Oaks, in Washington, D.C. (U.S.A.), a beautiful lawn on flat ground gives the illusion of greater length by descending in a series of steps and progressively narrowing at the far end.

Lawns look especially good when they have a sharply defined outline. For example, an ellipse or oval is a very attractive lawn shape. Square and rectangular lawns work well in formal gardens; kidney-shaped lawns are more desirable for an informal effect.

A grove of trees on a lawn can be a sensational feature, especially trees with richly textured trunks, pruned of lower branches. Lime trees, Scots pines and paper-bark maples are especially beautiful as lawn trees. They grow tall and if spaced sufficiently far apart will admit enough light for the grass to grow. Orchard trees like apples and pears can also make good lawn highlights, particularly when the branches are trained to make a weeping effect.

Lawns generally require "mower strips" wherever grass meets an obstruction or a barrier, such as a wall, tree trunk, or flower bed. A flat surface about the width of a brick is needed so the mower can cut a clean edge without the need to use tedious grass shears or power trimmers. In addition to brick sunk so the surface is level with the soil (to clear the blades), good mower strip materials include flat stones, Belgian block, and concrete tiles. Small landscape chips and wood-chip mulches are best avoided because the mower

blades and the wind velocity created by them can scatter pieces across the lawn. Garden peat, however, is more apt to stay in place.

There are many misconceptions about lawn grasses. It is best to disregard specific lawn varieties and consider only mixtures. A good formula for a hardwearing lawn on a sunny site will consist of several types of improved perennial ryegrass, and fescues. The improved perennial ryegrass is fast germinating and vigorous, helping to establish a new lawn with amazing speed. Improved perennial ryegrasses will ger-

Here is an example of Blue Rug creeping juniper used in a formal setting. Creating a carpet of ground-hugging evergreen foliage along a wall adjacent to a swimming pool, the blue hue complements the blue pool water.

In acid soils, where conditions are cool and moist, moss can substitute for grass. Here the moss even decorates the tops of stones by the stream running through an Oriental garden.

minate within three days and actually show green in five to seven days from broadcasting, or sowing, the seed. The introduction of these wonder grasses makes creating a new lawn from seed more appealing than laying sod, since the cost of sodding large areas can be prohibitively high and the time gained in comparison to the rate at which grasses can now grow is so slight.

Turf grasses in Great Britain can be classified as coarse-leafed and fine-leafed. Lawn mixtures for hard wear generally are a blend of both types, with improved perennial ryegrasses (a coarse-leafed type) the predominant variety. However, if a ''putting green'' or ''bowling green'' look is desired, then the mixture should contain only fine-leafed types such as fescues and bentgrass. It should be realised, however, that even a mixture of so-called coarse grasses can give a velvet-like, smooth texture providing that improved perennial ryegrass is the main component. The old standard varieties have a tendency to shred at the ends and look bleached after cutting with a lawn mower. If your mower blades are sharp, the new improved perennial ryegrasses will cut clean for an attractive appearance.

Lawn maintenance consists of watering during dry spells, mowing, applying fertilizer in spring and autumn, dethatching, reseeding bare spots (patching), adjusting soil pH (liming), and applying weedkillers when noxious weeds such as chickweed and dandelions take hold. Watering can be done with sprinklers, but for those who can afford it, the installation of an underground irrigation system, with sprinkler heads set flush with the soil surface so the mower blades clear them, is well worth considering.

Mowing is best done with the mower blades set high, since it is not so much the height of the grass that determines a lawn's good looks as the uniformity of cut. In any event, a thick lawn, evenly cut, is much better looking than a lawn clipped so low it glares at you. If you have time for applying fertilizer, seeding, or dethatching only once in a season, do it in the autumn. Fertilizing grass in the early autumn stimulates root growth and helps to achieve a flush of good green growth when warmer weather returns in the spring. Similarly, seed broadcast in autumn has little competition from weeds, and dethatching done then gives roots a chance to fill in where the thatch is removed before weeds can take a hold at the onset of spring.

For heavily shaded areas in woodland, where soil tends to be highly acid, it may be possible to establish a *moss lawn*. In less than ideal conditions, moss is extremely labour-intensive, requiring constant weeding to keep it from being suffocated. But where moisture is abundant under a good tree canopy in highly acid soil, moss can be sensational. In Japanese gardens,

TOP-RATED GROUNDCOVER PLANTS

Japanese Spurge
(Pachysandra terminalis)
Fleshy palmate leaves, evergreen

Myrtle
(Vinca minor)
Blue flowers, evergreen

English Ivy
(Hedera helix)
Evergreen

Plantain Lily
(Hosta species)
Blue, yellow, green, and variegated forms, flowering

Blue Rug
(Juniper horizontalis)
Evergreen

Rockspray
(Cotoneaster procumbens)
Evergreen, decorative berries in fall

Lilyturf
(Liriope muscari)
Variegated forms available, blue flowers

Algerian ivy
(Hedera canariensis)
Glossy leaves, good for slopes, tender

Bugle Weed
(Ajuga reptans)
Blue flowers, variegated forms

Dead Nettle
(Lamium maculatum)
Silver variegated form has yellow flowers

This famous lawn at Middleton Place Plantation, in South Carolina (U.S.A.), is terraced so that the setting sun makes striking shadows. There are four different water sources: the Ashley River (top), a pair of lakes laid out like butterfly wings, and a rice pond. The garden is strongly influenced by French landscape design.

where moss is a cherished groundcover, it is common for one or two gardeners to be employed for the sole purpose of maintaining the moss.

Groundcover plants fulfill several needs: (1) as a substitute for grass where grass will not grow, such as on steep, dry slopes and in shade; (2) as a labour-saving substitute for grass, since many groundcover plants never need mowing and make such a dense cover they deter weeds more successfully than grass; (3) to balance expanses of paving or to soften harsh lines formed by enclosures and paths; (4) to add textures and colours not possible with turf grasses. In addition to many gradations of green, there are groundcover plants that introduce silver, gold, lemon, blue, and other variation into the landscape.

The best groundcover plants are generally evergreen, or else they are deciduous plants that are so vigorous they can suffocate competition from weeds, such as hostas. However, some have special soil and light requirements, so care should be taken to match the right groundcover to the particular site. For example, in exposed sunny locations "Blue Rug" juniper, cotoneaster, heaths, ajuga, and liriope work well. In shade it's better to consider pachysandra, vinca minor, English ivy, hostas, and creeping euonymus. For sandy soils, camomile, sedums, gazanias, and ice plants—especially Hottentot fig—should be prime considerations.

In small gardens choose groundcover plants that stay within bounds. Pachysandra and vinca minor, for example, are well behaved and will generally stay within bounds with little more than a once-a-year trim around the edges.

Though most groundcover plants are chosen with no thought of flowers, there are some excellent flowering groundcover plants, sometimes referred to as "flowering lawns," which can add a little panache to these functional plantings. Pink-flowering English thyme is a good choice for sun, as are blue-flowering ajuga and purple-flowering liriope. Vinca minor will produce a good display of starry blue flowers in spring. Yellow-flowered celandine offers spectacu-

An edge of bricks helps a power mower make a clean cut of the grass without the mower wheels sinking into garden soil.

Facing page: *Hostas are popular groundcover plants, especially appealing when their beautiful leaf textures can be admired closely. Here the large blue and green leaves spill over a brick walk at the side entrance to a house.*

lar blooms in early spring, though it can be invasive, and lamium (dead nettle) offers bright yellow and purple flowers. Some of the hostas are not only spectacular in flower but are delightfully fragrant.

Many public gardens today are making a special feature of easy-maintenance groundcover plants. At the Royal Horticultural Society Gardens, near Wisley, Surrey, and the Royal Botanical Gardens, at Kew, near London, groundcover plants in immense variety can be found in garden settings. It is worth making frequent visits to these showplaces to keep abreast of new ideas in groundcover plants.

TOP-RATED TURF GRASSES AND TURF SUBSTITUTES

Brown top bentgrass

Camomile (herb)

Chewing's fescue

Creeping red fescue

Crested dogstail

Mosses

Perennial ryegrass (improved varieties)

Rough-stalked meadow grass

Thyme (herb)

Turf grass mixtures

The lawn at Cranbrook House, in Michigan (U.S.A.), features containerized camellias surrounding a statue, breaking up an otherwise monotonous expanse of lawn.

Facing page: This beautiful elliptical lawn, edged in boxwood, presents an attractive view from the balcony of a house. When seen from ground level, the lawn features as focal points a pair of topiary hemlocks flanking an eagle sculpture.

CHAPTER FOUR
ENTRANCES AND ENCLOSURES

This ornate gate of wood and wrought iron separates a lawn area from a flagstone terrace at Dumbarton Oaks, in Washington, D.C. (U.S.A.).

One of the most annoying experiences one can have when visiting a house for the first time is to discover there are three possible entrances—the front door, side door, and back door—with no clear indication of which door to use to announce one's arrival. People may even find themselves peering through windows, trying to determine the proper entrance. An entrance garden can indicate a main entrance. Also, a prominent path, beds of annuals, topiary trees in tubs, and pairs of sculpture are embellishments one can use to direct visitors to the main door. Similarly, the entrance to a garden can be clearly defined—unless the intention is to deliberately hide it.

For entry to a large garden, wrought-iron gates are impressive, announcing to the visitor that something expansive and exquisite lies beyond. For smaller gardens, however, fanciful iron gateways may be a little too pretentious, and a wooden gate or a door would be better suited to the garden. However, many fine gardens are approached by a simple gravel road disappearing over a hill or behind a line of trees, and this heightens the element of surprise when the garden comes into view. On the other hand, there are gardens with "false" entrances that are permanently closed, with the real entrance through a hidden side door or a gap in a hedge, the garden displaying its charms only to those who know the secret entrance.

Most often, garden gates are needed for security and privacy. Inside the garden more gateways may be needed to provide transitions from one area to another and also to frame a view, particularly when entering garden "rooms"—an enclosed garden space.

Doorways, gates, and arches are the principal *entrance-ways* the landscape architect employs to provide access to a garden or structure. Each kind of entrance achieves a different effect. For example, a solid door can be the best kind of security, especially when it is set into a wall, strong fence, or solid hedge. People approach closed doors with trepidation; there is often a feeling of trespass associated with doors you cannot see behind. A plain, solid door can also effectively screen out a service area; but if the door is the least bit ornate it can arouse curiousity. Solid doors can also act like a curtain to dramatically uncover some sensational feature, such as a shade garden or a parterre garden.

Gates, however, allow people to see over them or through them; they are polite alternatives to doors. Indeed, they say welcome in a dignified manner, encouraging people to open them and enter.

Arches evoke even greater feelings of freedom than gates. Just as water naturally flows through a gap in a dam, people are drawn instinctively to archways. There is no feeling of

This archway of hemlock beckons visitors into a rose garden.

This "tunnel" of hemlocks, their lower branches pruned away, acts as a dark corridor leading from one garden area to another at Old Westbury Garden, in New York State (U.S.A.).

Below: A "parterre" garden uses English boxwood to make miniature garden rooms, each with a tree-form rose in the middle. White gravel paths help to accentuate the outline of the hedges and also provide a cool, moist environment for the healthy growth of the boxwood.

This entrance to a suburban house features brick pillars with antique carriage lamps and a wrought-iron gate. Strap-like agapanthus leaves will look decorative even after the spectacular flowers have died.

Facing page: This walled garden at Old Westbury Garden, on Long Island, New York (U.S.A.), provides a perfect background for beds of perennials. Resembling an English manor estate, the garden has been described as being "more English than many English gardens."

restriction, and they are a wonderful feature for framing a spectacular view.

Walls, fences, and hedges are all *enclosures*—devices to screen things out or keep them in, depending on the situation. The Japanese and the British in particular love the idea of enclosing their garden spaces, for the tidy purpose of defining the cultivated area, for ensuring privacy, and in exposed areas, for establishing windbreaks. The Japanese like to be able to see beyond their garden enclosures, to take in a view of mountains or hills This concept even has a special word in Japanese garden design, *shakkei*, which means "borrowed landscape."

Walls can be used as barriers to lock out intruders. When the wall is high enough and solid enough it becomes difficult to climb and blocks out completely any hint of what may be beyond it. Brick and stone make good materials for walls. Low walls can be retaining walls—to prevent erosion—or they can be used to discourage people from accidentally stepping over a parapet or on to a planting area. Low walls can screen a ground-level feature such as a paved driveway or a parking area, yet allow vision beyond to an eye-level decorative feature.

Fences are less forbidding than walls. Made of wood or metal, fences can be constructed to obliterate an undesirable view or to be seen through. Fences and walls that have to negotiate a slope can present aesthetic problems. If the slope is gradual then fences can follow the grade, but even on gradual slopes walls are best constructed as sections that align the top parallel with the horizon, descending the slope in "steps." With fences, where a slope is steep, the fence can either descend in a series of panels with the top of each panel parallel with the horizon, or else a zigzag or "worm" fence can be used to negotiate the slope.

Fence designs are extremely important in establishing the overall style of a garden. For example, a bamboo fence can accentuate an Oriental influence; a picket fence can evoke the feeling of a seaside or English cottage garden.

Hedges are living walls that are restful to the eye, offering smooth contours. They can be trimmed low to define the edge of a walk or to bring neatness and order to a garden. When tall enough, they can also act as barriers and windbreaks. Indeed, hedges are much more successful at reducing the destructive force of wind than a solid wall or fence. A gale-force wind can strike a solid barrier (such as a brick wall) and jump right over it with equal—or even greater—force, but hedges cushion the force of the wind and dissipate its strength. Hedges can be created from various kinds of bushy evergreen or deciduous trees and shrubs. The advantage of evergreens is their unchanging quality. They are often referred to as the "bones" of a garden, giving it shape and form through all seasons. Deciduous hedges, even devoid of leaves, can still present a solid barrier, but tend to offer more interesting leaf patterns through the growing season. Also, some deciduous hedges—like forsythia and spitaea—offer spectacular floral displays.

When choosing hedges, the size, colour, and leaf texture is important. For example, English laurel is a popular hedge material in many gardens because the large, shiny jade-green leaves are highly ornamental. In cold climate gardens, beech and hornbeam are favorites because the serrated leaves and prominent leaf veins are appealing.

Most hedges must be trimmed at timely intervals to maintain a dense habit. The contour can be squared, rounded, or tapered. Windows and doorways can be cut into them. English boxwood is one of the few plants that can be left untrimmed to make a tight, billowing, informal hedge, since its growth rate is little more than one inch a year.

To make a dense hedge it is best to space plants close together at evenly spaced intervals—30.5 to 91.5 centimeters, depending on the variety. A sod-free area should be maintained around the plants so that water and fertilizer can be applied whenever necessary, and so that lawn mowers will not accidentally damage the trunks.

Smooth round beach stones make a strong wall at Carmel, California (U.S.A.).

A wall of pink stucco is decorated with espaliered Southern magnolia trees. The large, fragrant white flowers and waxlike, glossy green leaves make the magnolias an excellent choice for covering walls.

HEDGING & SCREENING PLANTS

*Box, English
(Buxus sempervirents)
Derse, evergreen, slow growth

Hornbeam
(Carpinus betuius)
Similar to beech but better in poor soils

*Leyland Cypress
(x Cupressocyparis leylandi)
Needle evergreen noted for fast, upright growth

Forsythia, Lynwood
(Forsythia x intermedia)
Sensational yellow flowers in early spring

*Holly, English
(Ilex aquifolium)
Spiny leaves, red berries on female plants

*Privet, Golden
(Ligustrum ovalifolium ''Aureum'')
Leaves have golden yellow centres

English Laurel
(Prunus laurocerasus)
Large, shiny evergreen leaves

*Yew, English
(Taxus baccata)
Needle evergreen, dense, slow growing

Barberry, Purple-leaf
(Berberis thunbergii atropurpurea)
Purple-red foliage, dense deciduous habit

*Escallonia
(Escallonia hybrids)
Masses of red flowers in spring

*Elaeagnus
(Elaeagnus x ebbingei)
Silvery foliage, scented white flowers

Burning Bush
(Euonymus alatus)
Brilliant red or pink autumn colour

*Evergreen

Euonymus japonica—an evergreen vine—helps to decorate a trellis fence in a Princeton, New Jersey (U.S.A.) garden.

The double hedge screens out a utility area at Blake House, in California (U.S.A.).

An American Colonial-style brick stairway provides a handsome change of elevation up a steep ascent.

This high stockade fence not only serves as a windbreaker, but also plays host to an assortment of flowering vines, including vining geraniums and weeping rosemary.

Facing page: *This wooden picket gate and matching fence introduce visitors to a small formal garden beyond.*

This wooden arched gate set into a dense hedge provides a good entranceway close to the street.

This royal coat of arms, set into a wrought-iron gate at the entrance to Kew Gardens, in England, signifies them as royal botanical gardens.

This style of rustic fence is a trademark of gardens in Carmel, California (U.S.A.).

The severe lines of this wooden lattice fence have been softened by vines and clumps of blue sea statice.

Facing page: A beautiful billowing hedge of English boxwood delineates a walk, leading the eye to an expanse of lawn bordering the Delaware River near Philadelphia, Pennsylvania (U.S.A.).

CHAPTER FIVE

SEATING AND VISTAS

An English-style teak bench provides a comfortable place to sit and a beautiful view from under an apple tree.

Seats provide both focal points in a garden and places from which to admire a view. Many gardens can be faulted for not providing sufficient places to sit. Not that every garden should have avenues of benches like a Continental municipal park, but most private gardens benefit from the strategic placement of seats, with special attention paid to their design and construction.

Places to sit in a garden can be provided without actually having a seat or a bench. The railing of a bridge can be made wide and low enough to offer a place to pause and sit at a jaunty angle. A low "sitting wall" with a wide, flat top can offer an inviting place to sit casually at the edge of a terrace.

Seats can be highly stylized or unobtrusively rustic, made of wood, metal, or stone—or a combination of all three materials. Teak benches have become extremely popular in recent years, some of them utilizing traditional designs from famous British gardens. The beige coloring of new teak weathers to a beautiful silver finish and lasts indefinitely. North America has produced some interesting styles of benches. Furniture makers in the Adirondack mountains, for example, produced a seat with a steep seat and a high reclined back. New England craftsmen make a rustic seat from pliable branches. From South Carolina there is the Charleston "Battery" bench—a combination of wooden slats supported by black wrought-iron end pieces, first admired along the waterfront sections of historic Charleston. Seaside gardens tend to favour white wicker, though it is perishable and not long lasting unless put under cover during winter. More durable are white metal seats, sometimes called "peacock" seats for their flared back and intricate designs. Made from woven wire, they are very popular in Victorian gardens.

Seats demand a planting strategy of their own. For example, ornamental seats look good against dark evergreen hedges or vines. Fragrant plants—especially those that hug the ground and release their fragrance when bruised by the tread of feet—can be planted between cracks in the flagstone of a sitting area. Camomile and thyme are examples. Similarly, fragrant flowers can be planted close by. Night-scented stocks and sweetpeas are perfect near a bench; also tuberoses and hyacinths. Honeysuckle makes a fragrant arbour over a seat, as do jasmine, wisteria, and sweet clematis. A sense of privacy and intimacy can be created by nestling seats into high hedges laid out in semicircles and horseshoe patterns. Seats and benches can be recessed into walls and hedges for more intimacy—or made so conspicuous that they become a focal point of the garden. Where spacious views are desired, a mature tree is a good place to position a seat that completely encircles the tree.

Garden seats are good for stimulating conversation and

Left: *Thomas Church designed this garden with ample room for sitting.*

Almost inconspicuous because of its small size, this tough little garden bench tucked against a brick wall at Filoli Garden, in California (U.S.A.), is a favorite spot for the gardeners to take a break.

provoking ideas. When a group of people withdraw from the confines and formality of a house to take a breath of fresh air in the garden, a cluster of comfortable seats positioned around a table introduces an air of informality, encourages people to be more frank, free-thinking, and inspirational. Many complicated ideas have been conceived in the sitting area of a garden. Darwin used his garden for inspiration when writing his *Origin of The Species,* and Newton was seated under an apple tree when he formulated the laws of gravity.

Other forms of repose to consider are swing seats, hammocks, and spring seats. Swing seats generally have a canopy over them and allow two people to sit side-by-side while the seat swings gently to and fro. Spring seats are usually made of metal or wicker and are shaped like a cocoon. The top is

A park bench, similar to the famous Charleston Battery bench, featuring cast-iron end pieces and wooden slats, provides a comfortable place to sit under the flowering canopy of an ornamental cherry in the author's own garden.

attached by a coil to a stout tree limb or a beam to allow one person to bounce up and down a few feet off the ground. Hammocks can be made of canvas or rope and are strung between tree trunks, stone pillars, or posts. Hammocks have a way of becoming the most popular resting place in a garden, especially when one can be positioned in a delightful grove of trees for cooling shade, or with an inspiring view such as a seascape.

*This dignified, comfortable seat in the gardens of the Govern-
or's Palace in Colonial Williamsburg, Virginia (U.S.A.), provides
a place to pause and rest.*

An English teak bench is firmly placed on a flagstone base, offering a spectacular view of a woodland garden.

This simple marble bench at Jasmine Hill Garden, in Alabama (U.S.A.), provides a good focal point as well as a fine view of a water garden.

Facing page: The beautiful, elegant contours of this wooden bench at Dumbarton Oaks, in Washington, D.C. (U.S.A.), echo the sweep of a background hedge and allow the bench to accommodate four persons, or more, with ease.

VISTAS

The most popular place for a bench is in front of a vista, whereby the eye is drawn to a distant scene or object. Vistas can be formed by corridors, by avenues, by the lay of the land. The French and Italians make vistas with trees in parallel lines. The most famous French avenues, called *allées*, are on level ground, but the most outstanding Italian examples can be seen on hillsides where steps may descend a slope to give the illusion of great distance. Usually a large sculpture or other ornate structure is sited at the end as a focal point.

English-style vistas are more informal, often cutting through natural woodland to a view of a free-form lake in the distance, or with a temple on a hillock as a focal point. To emulate these grand concepts of landscaping it is not necessary to own a large parklike estate. The principles can be applied to the smallest garden, using smaller trees and compact shrubs to delineate a narrow or short vista with a more modest focal point, such as a birdbath, garden seat, or gazebo.

Even in traditional Oriental gardens, where winding paths and zigzag bridges are used to create stroll gardens with many twists and turns to make maximum use of a confined space, the concept of a focal point is important. Favourite focal points of the Japanese are stone lanterns, bridges with high arches, earth mounds, boulders, and lone trees. The lone tree is often a pine, willow, or plum on a promontory or mound. Frequently the tree is pruned to simulate the weathered trees found on mountaintops in the wild. Limbs are removed between prominent scaffold branches and the remaining limbs bent or shaped with wires and splints until they assume artistic forms. In European and American gardens special weeping tree mutations—such as the weeping beech—are placed as focal points to symbolize cascades, fountains, and torrents.

The dazzling blossoms of a bougainvillea vine reflect the sun's rays, helping to create a spot to sit and suntan.

This is a close-up of the marble base supporting a seat at Hearst Castle, in California (U.S.A.).

Above right: This stone seat in Tresco Abbey Gardens, in England, uses quarry stone and a sacrificial altar, once used by Druids, as a picnic table, though most visitors are oblivious of the fact.

Tucked snugly into a secret garden, this pew-like bench is as comfortable as it is attractive.

CHAPTER SIX

WATER IN THE GARDEN

This small fishpond, with cherub fountain, provides a good focal point in this intensively planted English-style cottage garden.

Life on Earth began in water, and all life depends on it. In traditional Japanese gardens water—along with stone and trees—is considered the essence of great landscape design. All other forms of embellishment are merely incidental to these three key features.

Water is the magic of gardens. It is that special quality that gives them life, fills the air with nature's music, and dazzles the eyes with movement. Water is cool and flowing and works its wonder in many ways. The skillful garden designer can make water produce a wide range of sounds, from the relentless crashing of great sheets of water onto stones to an almost imperceptible trickling over pebbles. Visually, the effect of water is perhaps even more alluring. Still water is a mirror, sometimes so clear it disorients the viewer. It puts a moon and trees under our feet, which is why so many Japanese bridges have high arches that provide better views of the exquisite reflections of moon and stars, of lofty trees and waterside ornaments.

Still water, as in a pond, can be dark as night, stained by the tannin from tree roots. It can be clear as crystal on an overcast day, revealing schools of fish; bright blue on a sunny day; muddy and mysterious after heavy rain; obscured by leaves in the autumn; a dormant sheet of ice in winter.

After a pond, the next most desirable water feature is a stream. It can be slow moving and meandering with great "S" curves, or it can be fast moving and narrow with lots of riffles, rocks, and waterfalls.

Features for streams include bridges, observation platforms, dams with spillways, rapids, waterfalls, pebble promontories, and sandy beaches. The flow of water along a stream can be made to create what the Japanese call the music of nature, varying in tone from the quiet trickle of water over shallow rapids to the incessant cascading of water from a great height onto boulders. Water can be made to drip, splash, and gurgle. It can glitter like a thousand flashing lights or be slowed to a stillness that can create mirror-like reflections. Its surface can be dark and mysterious or crystal clear, allowing fish to be observed clearly beneath its surface.

A rill or a flume are also good features to consider for streams. A rill is usually a narrow, straight channel of water that leads from one water feature to another, usually connecting pairs of ponds, pools, fountains or waterfalls. A flume is like a rill, but generally wider, and may meander, usually connecting two large bodies of water and allowing the water to race along at a rate that can turn a waterwheel. Flumes can be cut out of the ground and lined with stone, or made of wood and raised off the ground on posts.

Waterfalls in themselves can take many forms. There are smooth falls that tumble generously in a wide sheet like a pane of glass, or they can fall sparingly, in strands that the Chinese garden masters call "silver threads." Water can be made to move to the left or the right by the careful placement of protruding stones and natural rock shelves to tumble the water, creating "broken falls" or the spectacle of multiple waterfalls.

This small Oriental garden features a lantern on the promontory and a school of goldfish. Landscape architect Hiroshi Makita designed this garden so that it could be transported if the owner decided to move.

A beautiful man-made waterfall dominates the Garden of the Groves, near Freeport, in the Bahamas.

This man-made torrent looks perfectly natural because of the artful placement of rocks, driftwood, and informal plantings.

Pools can be formal or natural. Formal pools are generally rectangular, circular, or oval in shape. They have well-defined edges—usually a raised edge for sitting, or even a balustrade for ornament and safety if the pool is deep. The geometric shape of a formal pool usually complements some strong architectural feature surrounding it—perhaps an enclosed courtyard or a wide terrace. Formal pools are favorite places to feature sculpture, but plants are generally used discreetly. Cherubs to pour water, frogs and turtles to spout water, a fountain to jet water into the sky, are common ornaments for formal pools. A single water lily in a submerged pot, a clump of stiff-leaved flag iris in a sunken tub, perhaps a pristine group of calla lilies—but the architectonic design of the pool is the most important factor.

With informal pools, nature's materials come into play. Rugged boulders, driftwood, masses of waterside plants, even a rustic dock or an observation platform are all important elements for an informal pool. Stepping stones can cross a corner, a small beach can be made from smooth stones or white sand, a promontory can feature a stone lantern...the possibilities are unlimited. A good way to introduce water into an informal pond is by a waterfall or a grotto.

On a smaller scale, a water feature can be nothing more than a stone with a depression for collecting rainwater, or a well head. Where water is totally absent from a garden, it's possible to make "imagined" water courses—dry ponds and dry streams—as the Japanese call them. The bottom of these dry water features can be filled with sand or round pebbles.

Two problems with any kind of pond are keeping it free of algae and preventing it from becoming silted up—choked with mud from runoff upstream. Moving water is easier to keep clear than still water, and the presence of a boat in the water can sometimes produce sufficient movement to stir the surface free of algae.

Oxygenating plants, such as myriophyllum, anacharis, and caboma, should be introduced to still ponds, especially if fish are to thrive. These plants stay submerged, with ribbon-like and feather-like leaves. With formal pools, the use of a recirculating pump may be necessary, to pass water through a filter.

Keeping ponds clear of mud is a tough problem. Upstream, retaining dams may be needed to trap the silt before it reaches the pond. However, the best solution is a "mud trap," whereby floating debris is diverted from the main flow by a screen and dumped into a deep pit. As the pit fills up, a backhoe is used to scoop it out of the pit.

Fountains are features that garden purists dislike. They are the product of a technological age rather than an age of naturalism. Except for geysers and coastal blow-holes that produce brief crescendos of spray, nature does not produce

This cloud-like, formal water-lily pool provides exquisite reflections.

elaborate fountain effects. However, fountains do have their place in gardens, particularly those that need a dominant feature—especially in formal gardens.

Perhaps the best reason for a fountain is to create a rainbow. This is done by arching a jet of water out over a pool so it fans out into a f ne spray before crashing on to rocks—or some other obstruction—to create even finer water particles. These droplets of water produced from this action will invariably create a rainbow on sunny days.

Fountain designs vary greatly according to style—from the traditional to the contemporary, though usually the materials are either metal or stone. A great many variations are possible with the jet—or jets—of water. They can be regulated to constantly play at a predetermined height, swivel to describe parabolas, and change heights. As gravity pulls the water back to earth all manner of catchments can be used to create a visual spectacle of splashing or flowing water.

A water-lily pond, with a map of Bermuda layed out in turf grass, is a big feature of Palm Grove Garden in Bermuda.

BRIDGES

*"I build a bridge as a rainbow...
not to walk upon...but still to cross."*

—Hiroshi Makita, Japanese landscape architect

The lines above, from a poem written to commemorate the completion of a garden project incorporating a reflecting pond and a rainbow bridge, point to the fact that bridges need not be built strictly for walking over. They can be placed in the landscape for purely aesthetic reasons. The high arches of Japanese "moon bridges" and "rainbow bridges" are often impossible to negotiate, but they provide strong focal points and symbolism. Nor is it necessary to have water running under a bridge. A ravine, dry water feature, or even a depression can be reason enough to place a bridge in the landscape.

Though arching bridges are probably the most popular—with wood, stone, or metal being the preferred construction material—bridges can cross in a flat span. Arched bridges are favored because they allow clearer observation of the surroundings and cause people to stop and look around and into the water below. Flat spans tend to hurry a person across. They are used most often to cross narrow gaps. A flat bridge can be raised above the path it connects, placed flush with the path if lawn tractors need to pass over, or placed below the level of the path so you have to step down to the bridge and up the other side (this is a good choice where a bridge at ground level or higher would obscure a view from another vantage point).

Above right: An Oriental-style bridge of flat spans crosses a wide expanse of swampy ground. The flat sections are stepped so the bridge can negotiate a slope.

A dancing fountain ringed with begonias, in summer, is a main feature of this shade garden. The gazebo in the background provides a touch of Victorian elegance.

Flat spans can be made more interesting by a zigzag placement of boards or by butting slabs in a staggered fashion. This causes a visitor to pause before crossing and to take the span slowly. A zigzag bridge can serve as an observation deck, inviting a person to sit and dangle feet into the water, stir the water with a hand, or even fish.

Some landscape architects try to make rules about the use of certain styles of bridges, calling for chunky stone bridges where the terrain is rugged and trellised wood bridges in woodland settings, but the introduction of a stylish bridge into a natural landscape or a rustic bridge into a formal landscape often works well enough to ignore any rules.

This white Japanese-style moonbridge crosses Bamboo Lake, a garden designed by the author for Magnolia Plantation, in South Carolina (U.S.A.).

Oriental and Spanish influences combine to create this distinctive water feature, designed by landscape architect Cevan Forristt.

PLANTS FOR PONDS AND STREAMS

*Arrowhead
(Sagitarria latifolia)

Candelabra Primula
(Primula japonica)

*Cattail
(Typhia latifolia)

Gunnera
(G. manicata)

*Flag Iris
(Iris psendacorus)

*Horsetails
(Equisetum hyemale)

Umbrella Plant
(Peltiphyllum peltatum)

Ostrich Fern
(Matteucia Pensylvanica)

Rodgersia
(R. pinnata)

*Pickerelweed
(Pentacleria cordata)

Siberian Iris
(Iris siberica)

Marsh Marigold
(Caltha palustris)

*Water Hyacinth
(Eichornia crassipes)

*Waterlilies
(Nymphaea species)

*Water Poppy
(Hydrocleys nymphoides)

*Water Snowflake
(Nymphoides peltata)

**Indicates plants that will grow with their roots
permanently submerged in water.*

The fountain at Holker Hail, in England, is a surprisingly formal touch in a garden that is essentially natural woodland with sensational plantings of rhododendrons.

A rustic waterspout pours water into a bucket. Water is recirculated by means of a small electric pump.

CHAPTER SEVEN

SHELTERS AND FOLLIES

This gazebo-style summerhouse offers a good view of a hillside garden. A cock weather vane, Victorian cupola, and container plants are decorative flourishes.

Even the buildings are a type of garden sculpture, enhancement for the setting rather than the dwellings they appear to be.... The focal point of the garden is a garden house, tucked snugly within paintbox-coloured flower borders and draped with a clematis vine. Inside it are nothing but a wheelbarrow and some garden pots.

—Anne Shultes, describing a country garden

Many people expect garden structures to serve some practical purpose, but in fact they can be incorporated into a landscape purely to look good.

Of course shelters find their way into a garden for a multitude of highly practical reasons. They can be places to take refuge during inclement weather (summerhouses and gazebos); coverings to break the rays of the sun and provide cooling shade (arbours, porticoes, and pergolas); refuges from noise and intrusion (alcoves and grottoes); a protected environment to grow special kinds of plants (conservatories, greenhouses, and lath houses). There are also animal shelters, boat houses, outhouses, pump rooms, springhouses, wellheads, and icehouses with distinctive architectural lines, which provide other forms of shelter.

This bathhouse in the form of a Greek temple creates an interesting focal point at the end of a lake vista.

This Victorian-style gazebo features a serpentine flower bed of red salvia, leading the eye along a vista to the gazebo.

As well as being functional and attractive as focal points, shelters can serve as places from which to admire a special view. They can also provide support for a variety of attractive vines, including climbing roses, clematis, honeysuckle, and wisteria. Some of the most appealing decorative vines to cover structures are creepers—English ivy, Virginia creeper, and Boston ivy, for example. These vigorous, fast-growing evergreen plants can completely cover a structure, with doors and windows kept clear by pruning.

Certain structures are currently so popular as garden embellishment, they deserve special emphasis:

Gazebo is a word derived from the English ''gaze about,'' meaning to pause and take in a scenic view. Thus the gazebo is a structure that usually offers shelter and is open on all sides to provide a beautiful view either in one direction or all around. However, gazebos can also serve as focal points in a garden, to be looked at, as well as to be looked from. They can do double duty as rain shelters and as places for people to congregate during a party or to sit for a private tête à tête.

When a gazebo is made more substantial, closed on several sides, with windows and shutters to keep out the weather and furniture to encourage an extended stay, it is usually called a *summerhouse,* which is not to be confused with a *springhouse.* The springhouse is usually a small stone building with a slate or shingled roof, dark inside, built over a natural spring for the purpose of producing a cool microclimate, like an icehouse, for storing perishable commodities in American Colonial days. Springhouses generally nestle into fissures, beside a stream or pond, and in American gardens are considered to be a decorative feature. Springhouses reflect a strong farm or pastoral environment, while gazebos and summerhouses tend to evoke a more romantic pleasure-garden atmosphere, with the design suggesting a period or theme. For example, a gazebo in the form of a watchtower on a cliff—for the purpose of whale watching or just staring out to sea—can give a garden a strong nautical flavor; a gazebo in the form of a pagoda or tea house, suggests an Oriental garden; a white gazebo with lots of gingerbread trim and latticework can instantly establish the tone of a Victorian garden.

While gazebos and summerhouses can be copied or adapted from many established styles (gazebos can even be ordered by mail), they do provide an opportunity for a garden owner to be innovative by creating a design of his or her own. This is particularly true of rustic gazebos made from rough tree trunks and tree branches, possibly using a distinctive indigenous tree species as the construction material.

Arbours, pergolas, and *porticoes* are all decorative structures that serve a similar purpose: They are embellishments to

Dusted by a light sprinkling of snow, this American Colonial-style gazebo with dovecote not only serves as a focal point at the end of the lawn, but also as a place to view a water garden.

VINES & WALL PLANTS FOR SEMI-SHADE

*Akebia
(Akebia quinata)
Fragrant reddish-purple flowers in early spring

*Wintercreeper
(Euonymus fortunei)
Dense leafy vining habit

Hydrangea, Climbing
(Hydrangea petiolaris)
White flower clusters in summer

*Ivy, English
(Hedera helix)
Dense, leafy vines, some variegated

Virginia creeper
(Parthenocissus quinquefolia)
Dark green leaves turn crimson in autumn

Boston Ivy
(Parthenocissus tricuspidata)
Lush green leaves turn maroon in autumn

Firethorn
(Pyracantha coccinea)
White flowers followed by orange or red berries

White Jasmine
(Jasminum officinale)
Fragrant white flowers in summer

*Camellia
(Camellia japonica)
Glossy green leaves, abundant flowers

Grape
(Vitis species)
Beautiful autumn colour, decorative fruits

*Evergreen

Facing page: This conservatory serves as a sun room, with furniture and house plants coordinated to make a pleasant living area.

passageways. In addition to providing a transition from one place to another, they are extremely good at framing a distant feature, as a picture frame does. The arbour can be a free-standing archway, or it can be butted against a fence, hedge, or wall. Recessed arches often include a seat across the back wall. Arbours are made for vines or creepers to cover them—climbing roses, clematis, and honeysuckle are favorite plants for arbours.

Arbours can also become tunnels. With metal arches to form the frames, plants can be trained along them, especially laburnum, wisteria, and Virginia creeper.

Pergolas are much more substantial. They generally have pillars to support flat beams overhead, feature paving underfoot, and may extend for long distances. They often support a multitude of flowering vines for a sensational tour-de-force of plant life—wisteria end to end, for example. Porticoes are breezeways connecting two doorways—a roofed-over walk from the house to a studio or utility room, for example. They frequently feature fancy wrought-iron grillwork and upright sections of trellis with vines clinging to them. They are favourite places to hang baskets. If the portico is on the crest of a hill it frequently has a spectacular view into the garden area or across open fields, and becomes a good place to position ornamental benches.

Greenhouses and conservatories can be introduced into gardens as wonderful decorative structures, either freestanding in a special section of the garden or attached to the house so the greenhouse or conservatory becomes an extension of the house itself.

Functionally, greenhouses and conservatories are places to grow plants in a controlled climate. Sometimes the purpose is to grow a wide assortment of plants; other times, to concentrate on gathering together an exotic collection of colourful genera, such as orchids, cacti, and bromeliads. Greenhouses generally are practical structures—normally freestanding since all-around light is better for plant growth than light from one direction, as in a lean-to structure. A conservatory, on the other hand, is usually an extension of a house. It can be a garden room with plants arranged for decoration in an atmosphere suitable for entertaining.

Unfortunately, by their very construction greenhouses and conservatories are not the easiest structures to fit comfortably into a garden. Vast expanses of shiny glass must be integrated into a pleasing architectural design. (Glass is preferred to plastic or fiberglass. It has much better light transmission, does not discolour, and so projects a more pleasing image.) Greenhouse frames can be wood, galvanized steel, or aluminium. Wood frames are best when made from redwood or another good quality hardwood since it resists rotting, but a more practical choice is aluminium, which is stronger than wood and never needs painting.

Many people like lean-to's because they can attach them to the house and use some of the house heat. Also, it is a space-saving design, which can add substantially to the value of a property.

Among freestanding greenhouse units there are traditional

A gazebo in the woods features a table and benches, inviting guests to wander from the house and look out over a hillside garden.

This lean-to greenhouse is shaded by the branches of a magnolia tree, seen here in full flower. Without plants partly obscuring the structure it could become an eyesore rather than the decorative feature it was designed to be.

and nontraditional designs. The traditional shape—straight sides and peaked roof—needs to be carefully situated so it doesn't stick out like a sore thumb. Landscaping around it—without cutting off precious sunlight—can soften the harsh lines. If the greenhouse is placed on a raised stone wall, the stone can help make the greenhouse an acceptable garden feature, and if flower beds can surround the base, the structure may look less austere.

Custom designs for greenhouses and conservatories are readily available. For the true enthusiast with no financial restraints, the custom-designed greenhouse or conservatory is the best choice for gardening under glass. Less ambitious gardeners can consider window greenhouses. Normally of aluminium construction, with glass panes, they project shelves of plants out into the light by a foot or more. They use heat from the house to protect the plants during cool weather and a fan to provide air circulation during hot days.

A magnificent dovecote decorates a stableyard at Middleton Place Garden, in South Carolina (U.S.A.).

Positioned at the entrance to a house, this arbour provides shade and supports flowering vines that have not yet reached the canopy.

An American Colonial-style outhouse becomes a decorative highlight when a brick path with parallel beds of silvery lamb's ears leads up to the door.

GARDEN FOLLIES

I have always been drawn to those unusual architectural fantasies called follies—those buildings commissioned by wealthy and either highly civilized or slightly mad persons who wish to have on their land a building which, though totally useless as a dwelling, is created simply to delight the senses of the owner.

—Brooke Astor

The term *garden folly* is applied to any architectural garden structure that produces some kind of extravagant visual pleasure. It is usually highly theatrical in aspect—a whimsical or oversized gazebo, an elaborate summerhouse, a tower or pagoda, a created ruin, even a mysterious grotto.

The dictionary definition of a folly is "the condition or quality of being foolish . . . also a costly undertaking having an absurd outcome." Garden follies do have a hint of foolishness, but in many cases they exhibit great style and a wonderful sense of humour rarely seen in gardens.

One of the most impressive garden follies in North America is the Crowninshield Garden, at Eleutherian Mills, near Wilmington, Delaware (U.S.A.). Though it is in a sad state of disrepair and presently closed to the public, awaiting restoration, the entire acre site is a replica of a Roman ruin, built on a precipitous hillside previously occupied by stone buildings used to store gunpowder. The original buildings were destroyed in an accidental explosion, and the subsequent owner, Frank Crowninshield, amused himself over several years by converting the foundations into classical ruins, with amphitheaters, reflecting pools, columns, terraces, and courtyards. There is even a secret passage taking visitors from one level of the garden to another.

Perhaps the greatest garden folly in the world, however, can be seen at Hearst Castle, at San Simeon, California (U.S.A.), where newspaper magnate William Randolph Hearst built a spectacular mountaintop retreat. The Spanish-style castle is surrounded by extravagant Italianate gardens which include an arbour more than a mile long, completely encircling the castle and large enough for a horse and rider to pass under. Roman bathhouses, sumptuous swimming pools, and priceless sculptures collected from all over Europe also are part of this extraordinary folly.

Completely covered with creeping fig, the pump house at Palm Grove Garden, in Bermuda, serves as a shelter from rain showers.

A grape arbour attached to a studio provides cooling shade in summer. Delicious bunches of grapes are a bonus.

VINES & WALL PLANTS FOR FULL SUN

Trumpet Vine
(Campsis radican)
Orange or yellow trumpet flowers in summer

Clematis
(Clematis species & hybrids)
Large flowers in shades of red and blue, plus white

Winter Jasmine
(Jasminum nudiflorum)
Bright yellow flowers in autumn or early spring

Passion Vine
(Passiflora caerulea)
Exotic blue and white flowers in summer

Climbing Rose, Iceberg
(Rosa floribunda)
Masses of large white blooms

Wisteria, Chinese
(Wisteria sinensis)
Purple and white flower clusters in spring

Russian Vine
(Polygonum baldschuanicum)
Masses of white flowers. Rampant.

Honeysuckles
(Lonicera species & hybrids)
Mostly red or yellow flowers, highly fragrant

California Lilac
(Ceanothus species & hybrids)
Blue-flowered upright shrubs for sheltered walls

Bittersweet
(Celastrus orbiculatus)
Decorative red berries in autumn

This garden house, inspired by a structure seen in Brittany (France), was constructed primarily to embellish the landscape, but also serves as a storage place for garden tools.

Facing page: *This arched grape arbour at Nemours Garden, in Delaware (U.S.A.), is especially enjoyable in autumn as the fruit fills the air with a delightful fragrance.*

CHAPTER EIGHT

ORNAMENTS AND FOCAL POINTS

Garden spaces featuring modernistic sculpture with flowing lines such as this piece are much mcre likely to gain approval from a wide audience than abstract sculpture with hard lines and geometric shapes.

After greenery, nothing, I believe, enhances a garden more than sculpture.

—Thomas D. Church, landscape architect

Most sculpture and other ornaments—such as urns, fountains, and even interesting pieces of driftwood and boulders—first found their way into gardens as focal points. They were objects of beauty or symbolism to focus the eye upon, either at the end of a vista, at the cross axis of a square or rectangle, or at the centre of a "cup."

The choice of a focal point—whether natural or artificial—should be made carefully, with particular attention to scale in relation to its position within the garden and to its surroundings. Artists tend to be sensitive to the possibility of plants overpowering statues and sculptures, preferring backgrounds of dark green evergreens, hedges, and brick walls. But this is not necessarily a good practice. In some sculpture gardens, the attempt to set the pieces apart so that there is no interference from colour is so strict it is almost annoying. Such places often cry out for a unicorn romping in a field of wildflowers, for a nymph statue recessed into a ruined wall garlanded with climbing roses, for a modernistic work of art to be set into the middle of a tulip or peony garden. In reality, many sculpture gardens are not gardens at all, but collections of sculpture, with a minimum of plantings merely to justify the term "garden" as a means of attracting visitors.

One of the finest examples of a harmonious blending of sculpture and plants is at Jasmine Hill, near Montgomery, Alabama (U.S.A.). Filled with beautiful examples of Greek and Roman sculpture, the woodland garden contains dozens of major historical pieces, each one a focal point in its own special setting. There are avenues of flowering cherries framing mythical lions, a rectangular water-lily pond with the head of a goddess at the far end, and handsome terra-cotta urns contrasting beautifully with the shiny, sinuous trunks of crepe myrtle trees.

Sculpture works particularly well as a focal point at the end of a vista, and as a whimsical surprise. At the Ladew Topiary Gardens, near Monkton, Maryland (U.S.A.), the owner set a sculpture of Adam and Eve in an orchard garden, Eve tempting Adam with an apple in a thicket of purple azaleas. In a sunken garden at Sezincote, Moreton-in-Marsh, Gloucestershire, a monstrous animated metal snake coils menacingly around a simulated tree trunk and spouts water. Appropriately, this dank, mysterious garden space, filled with moisture-loving plants, is known as the Snake Pool. Whimsical sculpture is particularly good at drawing attention away from something less attractive, like nearby utility lines or a glimpse of a busy

highway. Contemporary sculpture seems to work best in an uncluttered setting—displayed as a lawn highlight, in a niche or against an evergreen hedge.

At Hever Castle, in Kent, England, an area called the Italian Garden features a ruined wall with statues and artifacts displayed along its entire length, each piece set on steps against the wall, where alpine and rock plants provide masses of colour. Sedums grow out of cracks; climbing roses, honeysuckle, and clematis scramble along the top of the wall; and vining geraniums cascade out of urns—colour is everywhere. It is one of those rare examples where the maxim "Emphasis on everything is emphasis on nothing" does not apply, be-

This panther is on the prowl at Brookgreen Gardens, in South Carolina (U.S.A.), where sculpture and plants strike a perfect balance.

This small Buddha, set in a niche between evergreens, takes on a special aura of serenity when draped in a mantle of snow.

An ornate dovecote dominates a wildflower garden at the Ladew Topiary Gardens, in Maryland (U.S.A.).

Lamps and lanterns make excellent focal points. Here, a lamp standard of carved swans becomes an interesting focal point by day, as well as a source of light at night.

cause the wall and its terraces form a stage where the sculptures and plants become performers.

On a smaller scale, sundials, birdhouses, birdbaths and bird feeders, lanterns, and garden benches can serve as good focal points. Where a larger focal point is needed, consider a gazebo, a tower, a summerhouse, or a fountain.

Evergreen hedges are popular for creating corridors and avenues which draw the eye to a focal point. English box-wood is a favoured shrub for such a purpose. Slow growing and dense in habit, boxwood can be sheared to make clean, sharp lines like a wall, or be allowed to billow out, cloudlike, to form a more natural shape.

Many plants can be effectively trained over arbours, pergo-las, and archways to make a tunnel leading to a focal point—especially winter jasmine, trumpet vine, wisteria, and climb-ing roses. At Middleton Place plantation, in South Carolina (U.S.A.), mature camellias in parallel lines form long avenues. Their upper branches arch over gravel paths and intermingle to create a dark, eerie tunnel called a "ghost walk." Benches are positioned at each end as focal points and so that visitors

A simple birdhouse makes an appealing ornament in a tree.

can sit and contemplate the scene at leisure. In winter and early spring, when the camellia flowers drop their petals, the gravel paths appear to be covered with red confetti. In areas of Britain unsuitable for camellias, a similar effect can be created using rhododendrons. In addition to gravel, stone paving and brick can be important materials to enhance a vista ending in a focal point, especially effective on rainy days when wet stone and brick take on a shiny quality and become as much a decorative feature as the surrounding plants.

Some gardens trick the eye into making a distant focal point seem farther away than it really is. This technique is known as *trompe l'oeil*. A straight descent of steps is an effective device to give an illusion of greater distance. A lawn vista can be made deceptively longer by lines of trees in tubs, and by the lawn descending in a series of long terraces, each terrace becoming progressively narrower.

Trees and boulders can also serve as sculptural highlights to create dramatic focal points. Oriental gardeners are expert in using all kinds of trees as living sculptures. For example, a lone tree can be placed on a mound or a promontory, its form shaped like bonsai or topiary, by pruning and training, to create living artistry. Favourite tree species of the Japanese include gnarled ornamental plums, graceful weeping cherries, tortuous corkscrew willows, rugged-looking Japanese black pines, and spreading Japanese maples.

Interesting boulders can provide such effective focal points that the best landscape architects will scour quarries, rock-falls, and dry riverbeds for striking rock formations. Boulders as big as grand pianos were moved by the Japanese to create their exquisite imperial gardens in Kyoto. In the Sento Imperial Palace, egg-shaped cobblestones, used to make an expansive beach, were selected from a distant eastern town with the same care given precious stones. Wrapped individually in rice paper, they were valued at two litres of rice each. Moved by teams of mules and men, massive stones from remote hillsides were wrapped in quilts and straw overcoats by the Japanese to protect some delicate natural feature, such as a cushion of moss or a clump of ferns. Boulders that symbolized birds, animals, and mythical figures were especially prized and given names for the creatures they resembled.

Fortunate indeed is the garden that has a natural outcropping of boulders from which to make a strong focal point. At the Leonard Buck Rock Garden in Far Hills, New Jersey (U.S.A.), the most distinctive feature is a rugged cliff face that the late geologist, Leonard Buck, sharpened in outline by blasting and carving out ledges for rock plants to gain a foothold. Similarly, at the garden of the Henry Foundation, Gladwyn, Pennsylvania (U.S.A.), a massive rock outcrop at the crest of a grassy hill forms a sculptural highlight similar to Switzerland's Matter-

horn. Around its base, screes of limestone rock chips have been placed to provide sanctuary for rare rock plants, and trails with natural steps provide access to the peak. Native plants border the trails, and vines have been trained over some of the boulders to soften the expanses of rock.

Never underestimate the value of a good focal point to add distinction to a garden. The right choice of ornament, and a little imagination in siting and framing it, can make a mundane garden unique.

A pair of sphinx statues serve as silent sentinels at the entrance to a perennials garden.

Most gardeners like garden ornaments to be realistic. This lifelike deer statue, which is part of a cool water garden, is a good example.

This statue at Hearst Castle, in California (U.S.A.), takes on a sensuous quality, recessed into an alcove covered in flowering vines.

Below: *Many marble statues that once decorated Middleton Place Plantation were destroyed during the American Civil War by pillaging soldiers. This statue of a nymph tying her sandal was miraculously saved, however, and is so beautiful that it has become a trademark of Middleton.*

A touch of mystery and drama can be introduced to a garden by sculpture featuring mythical figures, death heads, and supernatural elements, particularly as a focal point at the end of a vista or inside a grotto.

Modern sculpture is often a controversial feature of gardens. A sculpture with flowing lines such as this one, however, seems to evoke less controversy than one with hard geometric shapes.

CHAPTER NINE

CONTAINERS

This Mediterranean-style urn, Pan statue, and stone seat decorate a sheltered nook at the end of a lawn vista, against a backdrop of hemlocks.

An incredibly diverse range of containers is available for growing plants, including urns, tubs, cauldrons, half-barrels, hanging baskets, and window boxes. Generally speaking, the larger and deeper the container, the more easily plants will grow in it, since shallow containers are prone to drying out too quickly. Hanging baskets, for example, may need watering several times a day in order to prevent wilting. Containers with drainage holes are also less trouble than those without. If you don't want to punch drainage holes in a container that doesn't feature them, then put a layer of aggregate such as broken clay pots or charcoal as a ''drainage ditch'' within the container. To prevent drainage holes from clogging with compacted soil, cover them with mounds of wire, rough stone, or convex pieces of clay pots.

Metal and plastic are the worst materials to use as containers unless some form of insulation is provided on the inside; metal and plastic both heat up quickly and can burn delicate root hairs by overheating the soil. Clay, wood, and ceramic containers are much better because they help to establish a cool environment inside the container. In general, one of the most important factors in choosing a container is its porosity. Clay is best, with ceramic and wood a close second and third.

It's a lot easier to purchase a ready-made potting soil for containers than to use garden topsoil or to make your own soil mix. However, a problem with many commercial soil mixes is that they tend to be unduly light in texture; they may not anchor plants successfully, and they may lose nutrients and moisture too rapidly. The most successful container-gardeners generally mix a little garden loam into packaged soil mixes to make them more substantial. A good do-it-yourself soil mix for containers consists of one part seived garden topsoil, one part sand, and one part peat, leaf mold, or well-decomposed animal manure.

This wooden fence is covered with metal brackets to hold an assortment of hanging baskets.

Facing page: *These vegetables are growing in raised beds. Increased soil depth improves drainage in an otherwise low-lying area, gives plants more room to grow larger yields, and makes care easier.*

Colourful crepe myrtle, resplendent in flowers, decorates a terra-cotta urn. Note how the tree is growing in a small utilitarian tub sunk into a bed of gravel inside the urn, so that before the first frost the terra-cotta urn and the crepe myrtle can be stored more safely in separate places.

Holding a planting of succulents, this magnificent cast-iron ornamental urn provides a strong focal point in a hillside garden, giving the garden a Mediterranean atmosphere.

These raised beds for vegetables are higher than normal so that people who are handicapped or elderly can cultivate them without bending.

Overlooking the St. James River near Richmond, Virginia (U.S.A.), this massive urn serves as a point of reference for visitors approaching the river. The urn also marks the end of a long vista, visible from the main house.

Agave mescal, a North American succulent, makes a dramatic highlight in a window-box planter mounted on a wall.

Watering is best done with long-spouted watering devices, applying moisture directly to the soil surface. Feeding can be done by mixing a diluted liquid plant food in with the water (read label directions for weak-strength applications), or by foliar feeding, whereby liquid plant food in a 1–2–1 ratio of nitrogen, phosphorus, and potassium (such as 10-20-10) is sprayed onto leaf surfaces for absorption into the plant.

Hanging baskets that are made of wire, with a layer of moist sphagnum moss forming a "nest" between the wire and the soil mix, are much less prone to dehydration than plain plastic baskets. Also, a more aesthetic effect can be obtained, since plants are easily poked through the sides to give the basket a fuller figure (although there are new plastic baskets with notches around the rim so plants can cascade more easily over the edges to make a rounded or columnar shape).

Raised beds should be considered wherever a difficult soil condition exists. If you have waterlogged soil, for example, or soil with impervious hardpan, a layer of crushed stone can be put down and a suitable topsoil carted in to make a raised bed above the indigenous soil. Landscape ties or stone retaining walls can keep the raised soil in place.

If you want to grow acid-loving plants in alkaline soils, and vice versa, raised beds are the answer, since it's a lot easier to bring in soil with the proper pH than to try to change the original pH with soil amendments.

Raised beds are also effective for growing fruits and vegetables in confined spaces, even where the natural soil is good. A soil area raised a foot or more gives food plants room for extra root development for maximum yields. Vegetables in raised beds are much easier to care for, as you don't have to stoop so far to do the weeding and harvesting.

To bring neatness and order to a garden, particularly a vegetable garden, raised beds can be layed out in squares, rectangles, and triangles to make interesting geometric patterns.

Tubs and window boxes are effective features for decorating patios, decks, terraces and entryways. Different floor arrangements can be made with tubs of varying heights and widths, while window boxes can be used on shelves and walls as well as window ledges.

CONTAINER PLANTS

There are many good reasons to grow plants in containers, but surely the best reason of all is the opportunity it provides to grow something outrageously exotic indoors during the winter cold, then move it outdoors in the spring to a place of prominence for the sheer pleasure of surprising guests. There is an elite group of mostly tropical plants that rarely fail to thrill even the most widely travelled visitor. These will grow quite easily in containers, and each possesses some special ornamental quality. Try them on decks and patios, or as sentinels to accent an entryway.

Angel's Trumpets
Datura suaveolens, with white flowers, and *D. sanguinea,* with reddish-orange flowers. Both form small trees, and generally flower the second year. Sometimes listed as B. Rugmansia.

Dwarf Bananas
Musa acuminata nana (yellow fruited) and *M. velutina* (pink fruited) produce lush tropical leaves that are reason enough to grow them, quite apart from the fact that they bear interesting fruit.

Bird-of-Paradise
Strelitzia reginae has paddle-shaped leaves and exotic birdlike orange-and-blue blossoms.

Top Hat Blueberry
This dwarf blueberry (*Vaccinium angustifolium*) stays neat and compact, looks like a well-trained bonsai, and almost smothers itself in edible fruit.

Citron

Citrus medica is an ornamental citrus, more striking than the usual Calamondin orange that is popular for pots. "Ertog" has large lemon-yellow pointed fruits bigger even than grapefruit. "Buddha's Hand" bears equally large aromatic golden-yellow fruit with astonishing finger-like protrusions.

Hibiscus

Hybrids of the Chinese hibiscus (*H. rosa-sinensis*) are everblooming and produce flowers up to 10 inches (25 centimeters) across in shades of yellow, orange, red, crimson, pink, and white. New dwarf kinds stay neat and compact.

Elephant Ears

Colocasia esculenta produces enormous heart-shaped leaves up to 5 feet (1.5 meters) long. Makes a fabulous highlight for a swimming pool.

Hawaiian Tree Fern

Cybotium glaucum is considered the most beautiful of all tree ferns. Its slender "fur"-covered trunk is topped with a fountain of lush feathery fronds.

Sago Palm

Cycas revoluta is not really a palm but a member of a much older family known as cycads, believed to be the oldest plant form on earth. The thick, dark trunk is crowned with a fountain of symmetrical dark green fronds.

Tree Tomato

Cyphomandra betacea has large heart-shaped leaves that smell like popcorn when rubbed. Edible plum-shaped red fruits hang in heavy clusters. The New Zealand hybrids flower and fruit within six months; wild South American species may take two years.

These pink geraniums decorate a horse trough. A metal plaque is set into a stone alcove for decorative appeal.

CHAPTER TEN

RECREATION AREAS

This large pavillion at the head of a swimming pool provides plenty of space to entertain guests under cover.

Play areas in a garden can be categorized into two types—play for young children and play for adults. Play areas for children are generally quite conspicuous—usually within sight of the kitchen window. The components that make up the play can be conveniently grouped together—for example, a sandpile, a wading pool, a swing and slide set, even a seesaw and playhouse.

Less conspicuous play features for young children can include a climbing tree, specially pruned and adapted to make climbing safe and easy, a hollow tree, a tree house, a sandy beach adjacent to a shallow pond, a wading pool that doubles as an ornamental fountain or reflecting pool. Children also enjoy feeding fish in a water-lily pool and catching fish from a dock over a shallow pond or from a bridge over a stream.

Wherever children are expected to play, it's essential to provide a soft surface to cushion falls. Wood and aluminium construction is preferable to stone or steel. A groundcover of grass or spongy garden peat is better than concrete or flagstone.

Both children and adults like places to kick balls, throw Frisbees, and play lawn games such as horseshoes, shuttlecock, volleyball, and croquet. For these areas a hard-wearing lawn grass is needed, such as perennial ryegrass. Grassy play areas can be made to look attractive by enclosing the edges with a low hedge of boxwood or bayberry, by shaping the area into an oval, ellipticle or kidney shape, or incorporating the play space into a vista. A decorative playhouse with a table tennis or billiard table is a good place to store sports equipment.

A small basketball practice court can double as a place for children to ride tricycles, skateboards, and rollerskates. The problem with children's play areas is how to make them attractive garden features. Obviously, a flimsy metal jungle-gym purchased from the local discount store is going to be an eyesore, but attractive play sets made from treated pine enclosed by a picket fence or a low hedge can be a decorative feature. A good selection of these can be found usually at a specialist in fencing materials, with several sample units on display. The trick is to make the play space look more like a landscape garden feature and less of a playground. This can be done by making it look like a Spanish-style plaza, a stableyard or courtyard, with tiles, brick or flagstone used to effect the illusion. A cycle track can completely encircle an oval or ellipticle lawn and look like an innocent paved footpath, yet provide a continuous circuit for children to ride or skate.

More suitable for adult play are a jogging track, a putting green, a croquet lawn, a tennis court, or a Jacuzzi. Jogging

When covered in vines, a brick barbecue becomes a decorative garden feature.

A path with long, straight sections does double-duty as a means of negotiating a steep slope and as a jogging track for the owner.

tracks have become a popular feature of college gardens and large estates, but one can be incorporated into quite a small area—an acre—by making the track skirt the boundary of the property. On a site with a steep slope the track can zigzag down the slope in a long path that makes hairpin turns.

Swimming pools are, without doubt, the most popular recreation feature in a garden. Most are situated out in the open, though some are in special pool buildings. The benefit of a pool building is that a pool can be used over an extended period and requires much less maintenance, such as cleaning and winterizing; the building also provides greater safety.

Swimming pools can be informal or formal. Informal pools are usually free-form, such as a kidney shape, and feature boulders, driftwood, and plants in close proximity. Usually the informal pool recirculates its water by means of a waterfall, which can be high enough to swim under. Water can also be

arched into the pool by means of converging jets, and by overflowing from a fountain. The largest free-form pool in the world is located at the Hotel Cerromar in Puerto Rico. Over a quarter of a mile long, it includes naturalistic water slides, grottoes, and lagoons.

In parts of the world where an outdoor swimming pool can be used more than six months of the year, there is good reason to make the pool a dominant feature, within sight of and easy access from the living areas of the house. In other sections of the country, where only a few months are considered to be the swimming season, it is better to locate the outdoor pool in a special screened area so that the empty winterized pool does not become an eyesore.

The placement of a pool is critical to its success in other ways. A sunny location will help heat the pool more quickly and avoid litter from falling leaves. Seclusion also helps make a pool more enjoyable—an attractive plant-covered wall or a windbreak of evergreens will not only make the pool environment more comfortable, it can screen out the vision of curious neighbours.

Paving of flagstone, brick, or concrete as well as wooden decks are good surfaces to use to surround the pool, to make a lounging area and to help keep debris, such as grass clippings, from blowing into the pool.

The most popular colour for a swimming pool is blue, and that is the colour you get with a white painted pool because of the reflection from blue skies. Green is a poor colour for pool water because it looks as if it is stained with algae. However, a very good alternative to blue is eggplant, or aubergine, particularly with informal pools.

Swimming pools are perfect places to decorate with container plants. Around formal pools, topiary trees in square wooden planters can look sensational. Less dignified, but more colourful, are flowering annuals in tubs, cauldrons, urns, and half-barrels. For informal pools, an exquisite tropical effect can be obtained by using elephant-ear caladiums, rainbow-leaf caladiums, monstera plants, dracaenas, yuccas, calla lilies, spathyphillums, and Verona ferns.

A rope swing takes advantage of a strong tulip poplar limb to provide unobtrusive play for both children and adults.

The edges of an outdoor jacuzzi have become a perfect setting for a collection of dwarf conifers, referred to by the owner as his "horticultural zoo."

Facing page : *The plain shape of a rectangular swimming pool becomes a decorative garden feature in a sunken setting at Dumbarton Oaks, in Washington D.C. (U.S.A.).*

This swing seat made from redwood provides a place to relax.

A rustic swing seat overlooks a stream in a garden.

Left: *This croquet court bordered by high topiary hedges is a perfect place to play on a sunny summer's day.*

CHAPTER ELEVEN

PLANTS AS FEATURES

Landscape architect Hiroshi Makita incorporated azaleas, dwarf bamboo, and ferns to accentuate an Oriental garden built around a rocky stream, where stepping stones follow the flow of the stream as a short cut from one garden space to another.

A prominent landscape architect walked into a beautiful English perennial garden during its peak of bloom. His immediate reaction was "All I see is plants. Where is the design?" On the other hand, people will look at a highly landscaped garden, one with lots of evergreen groundcovers, expanses of flagstone, low hedges, and gravel paths and proclaim, "Where are the plants?" Many landscape architects today design purposefully for low maintenance—with a deliberately low number of flowering plants—because they know that the owners will not take care of them. Unfortunately, most people expect to see flowering plants dominate a garden, and the gardens that combine flowering plants with a strong sense of design are few and far between. One of the finest partnerships in garden design occurred in England between Sir Edwin Lutyens, a brilliant architect, and Gertrude Jekyll, a brilliant plantsperson. Lutyens brought to the residences he built a strong sense of garden design, while Jekyll filled them with colourful plants. Her sense of effective colour combinations and companion plantings was sensational, made all the more dramatic—it is said—by her poor eyesight, which made her think more in terms of colour swatches than the refinements of a particular plant.

A double perennial border features grass used as a path down the middle.

COLOUR GARDENS AND OTHER THEMES

Flowering plants are not essential for every kind of theme garden—sculpture gardens are an obvious example. But colour gardens in particular call for mixing many varieties of plants and seeing how well they perform together. About her famous white garden at Sissinghurst, Vita Sackville-West wrote: "It is amusing to make one-colour gardens. . . . For my own part I am trying to make a grey, green and white garden. This is an experiment which I ardently hope may be successful, though I doubt it. One's best ideals seldom play up in practice to one's expectations, especially in gardening. . . . Still one hopes." Her doubts were ill-founded. In actuality, the white garden became one of Sackville-West's supreme triumphs.

White gardens are sometimes called "moon gardens," with white night-flowering plants added for extra dramatic appeal (moonflowers and night-blooming cereus, for example). They are particularly beautiful when seen at dusk or by moonlight. "I cannot help hoping that the grey ghostly barn owl will sweep silently across the pale garden next summer in the twilight," wrote Sackville-West of her white garden.

Gardens that create a special environment not only require plants that look well together visually, but also plants that thrive in similar conditions. Bog gardens, rock gardens, desert gardens, alpine gardens, shade gardens, and woodland gardens can draw on a wide selection of plants. Shade and woodland gardens rely heavily on ferns, desert gardens on cacti and succulents; bog gardens need plants that tolerate wet feet—flag iris, candelabra primulas, and water-lilies, for example. Theme gardens of all one plant family are especially romantic, though few plant collections of one genus provide colour for more than three or four weeks. Rose gardens are a notable exception. By skillful cultivation practices (such as irrigation, dead-heading, and a mulch material to keep soil cool), rose gardens can provide colour from late spring through autumn in a sunny location. A fern garden is a good choice for a shaded site, providing a cool green highlight for a prolonged period. Iris gardens and peony gardens, on the other hand, provide a short season of colour. For this reason they tend to be smaller and tucked away into areas where lack of colour for most of the year is not objectionable. If the area has a strong design, the dominent design element can make up for the absence of colour during nonflowering periods.

ARISTOCRATIC TREES

Cut-leaf Japanese Maple
(Acer palmatum ''Dissectum'')
Billowing habit, good autumn colour

Weeping Cherry
(Prunus subhirtella ''Pendula'')
Cascading branches covered in pink blossoms in early
spring

Weeping Willow-leaf Pear
(Pyrus salicifolia ''Pendula'')
Elegent tree with graceful silver-blue leaves

Dove Tree
(Davidia involucrata)
Lovely flower-like bracts cover the tree in spring

Snowdrop Tree
(Halesia monticola)
Masses of bell-shaped flowers in spring

Weeping Crab-apple
(Malus ''Red Jade)
Compact habit, pink flowers, red fruit

Honey Locust, Sunburst
(Gleditsia triacanthos ''Sunburst'')
Golden yellow young foliage turns light green

Dawn Redwood
(Metasequoia glyptostroboides)
Fern-like foliage turns golden in autumn

Dogwood, Korean
(Cornus kousa chinensis)
Masses of white flowers, strawberry-like fruits

*Holly, Blue
(Ilex x meservae)
Blue-green spiny leaves, abundant berries

*Evergreen

Above right: *A grove of redwoods displays textured, tall, straight trunks, creating a miniature forest within a coastal garden.*

The English foxglove and Siberian iris are perfect companions in a perennial flower border in front of a country cottage.

TYPES OF PLANTS

Annuals are plants that complete their life cycles in a single year. They tend to be the most colourful of all plant groups, and their colour displays are the longest lasting. Started from seed or purchased as bedding plants from local garden centres, many annuals will flower continuously for eight to ten weeks, providing a quality called "perpetual colour." These include alyssum, ageratum, wax begonias, calendulas, coleus, cleome, dusty miller, geraniums, impatiens, marigolds, multiflora petunias, scarlet sage, and zinnias.

Most annuals prefer full sun, but begonias, coleus, and impatiens will tolerate some shade. A favourite way to use annuals is to crowd them into beds and borders. In formal gardens, single colours are preferred, but for informality, a mixed bed—or a "rainbow border"—is effective. Also, mixtures of tall-growing annuals are good for "cutting gardens," whose purpose is to provide armloads of fresh flowers for the house. Annuals are easy to care for. They are generally pulled up after frost and the ground replanted in spring.

Annuals are popular components in wildflower mixtures to make fast-flowering wildflower meadows. The ground is turned over in spring and the seed broadcast. Cornflowers, Shirley poppies, gaillardias, calliopsis, feverfew, and cosmos are commonly used to provide essential colour the first year until perennial wildflowers have a chance to become established, blooming during the second season.

Perhaps no other flower class is more favoured for container features than annuals because of their everblooming quality. Favourite container annuals include alyssum, begonias, coleus, dusty miller, geraniums, impatiens, lobelia, marigolds, pansies, and petunias.

Perennials are a lot more trouble to grow than annuals. They generally produce only leafy growth the first year, lie dormant over the winter, and flower the second season. After the second season, most will continue to flower each year, providing they have been staked, fertilized, watered during dry spells, thinned, weeded, guarded from pests, and mulched during winter to maintain their vigor. The mixed perennial border has become more popular in recent years, though certain perennials are so spectacular they deserve special beds all to themselves—particularly peonies, daylilies, Oriental poppies, chrysanthemums, bearded iris, and primulas. Most perennials prefer full sun, though a few will take shade, including hostas and garden lilies (*lilium*).

Clumps of bearded iris line the banks of a stream. These summer perennials are one of the few plant families with sufficient range of colour to create a "collection" using a single genus.

One of the most sophisticated plantings is a double border of perennials. This usually consists of parallel borders backed by high hedges of cypress or a similar evergreen backdrop and separated by a broad, grassy path, or by flagstone. Since most perennials flower for only brief periods (two weeks on the average), the best perennial borders are planned to give maximum colour at a particular time of year—usually the middle of July, with token bursts of colour preceding and following the big splash. When an attempt is made to provide continuous colour with perennials, the colour display can be weak—unless lots of perpetual-flowering annuals are mixed in to help strengthen the floral display, which is what Gertrude Jekyll liked to do.

Flowering bulbs are often grouped with perennials in the garden. Two extremely useful types of bulbs for garden features are daffodils and tulips. They are star performers for early spring gardens. The advantage of daffodils is that they will come up through the grass, and flower every year. If fed with a high-phosphorus fertilizer twice a year—in spring before the plants bloom and again in autumn, after frost—they will multiply freely. Daffodils are spectacular when planted in drifts at the edge of the lawn or along slopes; they are also exquisite under deciduous trees in a woodland, completing their flowering display before the trees are in full leaf. Another classic use of daffodils is to crowd them along stream banks in generous clumps.

Tulips are poor for naturalizing, but wonderful in formal beds and as borders of all one colour or mixed. They generally require planting anew every year, since the bulbs fall prey to rot and hungry rodents, whereas daffodils are naturally repellent to pests and much less temperamental. Perhaps no other flowering plant has the range or the intensity of colour possessed by tulips. There are many flower forms—from the water-lily group with petals that unfold flat in full sun to the double "peony-flowered" group. The brightest and boldest colours are found in the relatively new class known as Darwin hybrids.

Shrubs bridge the gap between perennials and trees in the garden. Collectively, trees and shrubs are known as "woody plants" for their strong, durable cell structure, which gives them endurance and longevity. Shrubs are used not only for the ornamental value of their flowers, leaves, and the shapes they can be pruned into, but functionally as hedges, living walls, windbreaks, screens, and backgrounds. Shrubs and trees fulfill very different functions in the landscape. Shrubs are mostly used at eye level; trees are valued more for skyline effects. They become perfect companions when the trees form a canopy underplanted with ornamental shrubs, such as a grove of tall pines over a mass planting of azaleas.

An orchard of olive trees planted in regimented rows brings a touch of the Mediterranean to this garden.

All the flowers in this border are shades of yellow, creating a "single colour" theme garden.

Shrub borders in North America are not nearly as common as borders filled with perennials or annuals, since they require more space and care, but in Europe most large gardens feature a mixed shrub border. A very fine example called "the green garden" can be seen in the garden of Andalusia, near Philadelphia, Pennsylvania (U.S.A.). In addition to a fine collection of dwarf evergreens in different shapes and gradations of green, it includes a good assortment of flowering shrubs—notably Spanish broom, deciduous azaleas, rhododendrons, hydrangeas, viburnums, dogwoods, and a beautiful section of boxwood hedge leading the eye towards luxuriant lawns that sweep down to the Delaware River.

The value of boxwood should never be underestimated. For example, the combination of boxwood, flagstone, high shade, and an expanse of green lawn creates one of the most incredibly cooling environments. This cooling effect is a prime reason for the popularity of boxwood gardens throughout the southern United States.

Two other important groups of shrubs are rhododendrons (which include those small-leaf rhododendrons known as azaleas), and camellias. Rhododendrons (particularly azaleas) are so colourful they can establish a garden's reputation, particularly when the azaleas are used on hillsides in drifts, like daffodils except on a grander scale. Each year, visitors swarm to Charleston (U.S.A.) and other Southern cities in the spring to witness the azaleas in bloom. (Hardy varieties will bloom well into Canada and are popular in Europe.)

The Japanese refer to camellias as "living jade," for the extraordinary beauty of the glossy green waxlike leaves, which is enough reason to grow them. But then there are also the gorgeous flowers which generally appear very early in spring. They are captivating, with their smooth, rounded petals and heavy substance. Camellias frequently form "collections," and make exquisite tunnels and espaliers because of their pliable branches. Where winters are severe it is worth growing camellias in tubs and setting them outside after frost.

Trees are the most dominant life forms in the environment, and their presence in a garden can establish a sense of place better than any other type of plant. Weeping willows, with their billowing shape and swaying branches, can suggest the presence of a water feature; the rugged silhouette of Japanese black pines, a coastal garden; swaying palms or a grove of cycads, a tropical paradise. More than any other plant, trees can improve the cash value of a home; just one mature tree on a property can give other landscaping and plantings the look of maturity and character.

Trees and shrubs are classified as *deciduous* or *evergreen*, with evergreens further divided into "broad-leaf" (hollies, rhododendrons) and "needle" (pines, hemlocks). In Oriental

This herb garden features different species laid out in elaborate ribbons or knots.

gardens three-quarters of the trees may be evergreen, with deciduous trees introduced sparingly to provide an exotic blossom display in spring (such as cherries and crabapples) or to provide some vivid autumn colouring (ginkgos and Japanese maples). Evergreens are popular in gardens with a strong design because they bring permanence to the planting and give the garden structure through all four seasons. However, the British style of naturalism tends to favor the planting of deciduous trees. Leafless trees in winter have a special beauty in the tracery of branches etching wintry skies, and leafless trees in early spring permit the underplanting of forest wildflowers and flowering bulbs, which would not receive sufficient light in a woodland of evergreens.

Some fine examples of woodland gardens can be seen at Bodnant Garden, Colwyn Bay, Wales; Holker Hall, near Grange-over-Sands, Cumbria; Leonardslee Garden, Horsham, West Sussex; and Exbury Garden, near Beaulieu, Hampshire.

There are many other spectacular uses of trees in the landscape. The formation of avenues is particularly impressive when a single tree species is used to edge a driveway or a broad walk. A breathtaking vertical accent can be achieved with fastigate (upright) trees. The Lombardy poplar, and Skyrocket juniper are good examples of fastigates, which should be considered.

Vines make spectacular vertical features. They do to walls, fences, and posts what groundcover plants do on a horizontal plane. Most of all, vines help to soften large monotonous expanses of masonry or wood. However, some vines are more adept at climbing than others. Support—such as a trellis—is sometimes needed to keep a vine climbing against a pole or wall. The climbing mechanism used by a vine is very important in fitting it to a particular situation. Some have a twining habit (like clematis) that requires a netlike support to weave in and out of. Others have suction pads or aerial roots at each node (ivy and trumpet vine, for example), allowing them to grasp hold of hard surfaces like brick, cinder block, and stone. Still others, such as grape vines, have tendrils that do a good job of scrambling up poles and over arbours. Climbing roses is a misnomer. Their only means of climbing is the thorns on their long whiplike canes. Unless the canes are held firmly against a support with twist-ties or string, they will fall down. The Lady Banks and vigorous floribundas like Iceberg are more adept at climbing, for their canes form a tangle that allows them to climb up into trees and over bushes.

Vines such as Boston ivy and Virginia creeper are popular for covering large expanses of wall because the dark green leaf pattern in summer is appealing and in autumn turns to molten red. The yellow-flowered winter jasmine and common white jasmine are reasonably hardy and easily grown in most fertile soils. Clematis and wisteria are wonderful for their spectacular floral displays in spring, and wisteria also has a pleasant, heavy fragrance.

Honeysuckles, too, are popular for their delightful fragrance that carries long distances, but both wisteria and honeysuckle can strangle a young tree if left unchecked. The warmer the climate you live in, the more exotic your choices of flowering vines. In sheltered sunny sites along the South and South-West coast more exotic vines can be considered, such as the blue passion vine, blue potato vine and kiwi vine.

The choice of supports for vines is limited only by your imagination. Popular structures include arbours, gazebos, arches, towers, trellises, fences, grillework, dead and living trees, even balustrades. There are vines that can completely cover a small structure such as a pump house or toolshed.

Lovely white calla lilies contrast well with the muted colors of a stone dovecote.

PRUNING FOR DISPLAY

Topiary, espalier, and *bonsai* are all methods of pruning and training plants to achieve special effects. Though topiary—the art of pruning trees and shrubs into different shapes—was first practiced by the Romans, the British have produced some of the best examples of topiary gardens in the world. At Levens Hall, in the Lake District, there are examples of topiary work nearly three hundred years old.

Even a single piece of topiary can make a wonderful focal point. Choice plants for topiary work include Japanese and English yew, hemlock, boxwood, holly, and privet.

The best topiary gardens in the United States can be seen at Green Animals, near Newport, Rhode Island, and the Ladew Topiary Gardens, near Baltimore, Maryland. Particularly impressive at Ladew are immense hedges with windows cut into them and topiary figures in the form of swans riding along simulated waves.

Bonsai is the art of dwarfing plants by selective pruning of branches and roots, and by restricting the growth of their roots in special shallow containers called bonsai trays. The older a bonsai looks, the greater its aesthetic value. Bonsai masters have the ability to take quite young trees, prune away excessive branches, and wire them into special positions so they look as though they have been sculpted by the elements. The best bonsai are all intended to be exhibited outdoors, and they make exquisite focal points when placed on a wall, table, or pedestal.

Espalier involves training pliable branches, usually of fruit trees, onto a flat frame or against a wall. Those grown horizontally, along wooden rails or wires, are called *cordons*—a French word meaning "rope." Espaliers save space for growing fruits such as peaches, pears, and apples. They also can form a fence bordering a garden, though provision must be made to keep deer away from them. Espaliers can dress up expanses of wood or brick, but the fruit trees generally have a hard time contending with highly reflective walls, which may produce problems from dehydration and sunscald. For problem walls, a better choice is an ornamental espalier such as firethorn, English ivy, camellia, or magnolia.

Other less common methods of training trees and shrubs include *pleaching* and *pollarding.* The word *pleach* means "to weave" and indicates a double line of trees that have their branches woven together to create a tunnel. Pollarding involves pruning away the lower branches of a tree to a single

trunk and "topping" the crown. This encourages the growth points at the top of the trunk to produce an abundance of top growth. This flush of new bushy growth can be shaped into spheres and squares. Pollards make effective avenues and sentinels on either side of an entranceway and form a decorative rim around a courtyard.

Orchards bring to mind vast acres of flat ground with monotonous rows of fruit trees, but actually an orchard can be made in a small space by using special dwarf varieties. Orchards also can be under-planted so they are filled with colour at certain times of the year. For example, in an apple orchard daffodils can be planted so they bloom simultaneously with the apple blossoms. Bill Frederick, a landscape architect living in Delaware (U.S.A.), chose pink-flowering apple varieties to enhance the display in his orchard. But surely the most sophisticated orchard planting of all is a *nuttery* (a collection of nut-bearing trees) under-planted with snowdrops, aconites, primroses, and bluebells.

Herb gardens are currently enjoying immense popularity not only because herbs can be decorative, but because they provide such a wealth of useful products from herbs and spices to flavour foods to remedies for the relief of ailments, fragrances for potpourris, and natural dyes. Perhaps the most popular use of herbs is in a cartwheel design. Usually an ornamental feature serves as a focal point at the centre of the garden. Typically, this can be a beehive, a sundial, a birdbath or a sculpture. From this paths radiate out like the spokes of a cartwheel and groups of herbs are planted in the triangular beds between the spokes. The outside edge can be square, rectangular, or round.

Another favorite feature with herbs is a knot garden. This uses ribbons of herbs to create a design, usually of scrolls and flourishes. Herbs of contrasting colours are used to make the outlines. Popular choices are blue-leafed rue, grey-leafed santolina, red-leafed dwarf barberry, dark green thyme and other bushy, compact mound-shaped leafy herbs that can be trimmed low.

Chinese juniper has been pruned in topiary fashion to create a dramatic highlight at the corner of a lawn.

CHAPTER TWELVE

STORAGE AND SERVICE AREAS

This garage disguised as a stable makes a structural highlight out of a utilitarian storage space.

Gardens attached to houses should provide discreet areas to accommodate all kinds of paraphernalia, from tools to rubbish. Unfortunately, many people try to make the garage an all-purpose storage area, yet special facilities to take care of work materials and waste are generally easy and inexpensive to construct and to blend into the landscape or turn into attractive features.

A bougainvillea vine decorates a wooden fence used to screen off a utility area.

CAMOUFLAGING UTILITY AREAS

Sometimes it is possible to construct utility buildings so they are architectural delights and pleasant garden features. A garage can be made to look like a stable, boathouse, barn or carriage house. Materials such as old barn siding and shingles can be used to give a building a weathered look. At the other extreme, a quaint, colourful gingerbread structure might be preferred using fanciful adornments such as cupolas and elaborate trim.

Other times—especially in small suburban and city gardens—the presence of a neighbour's utility building may make it difficult to alter the basic structure and the best that can be done is to camouflage the offending wall. For example, if a neighbour's workshop backs onto your property, presenting a solid expanse of utilitarian wood siding or stucco, it may be quite easy for you to put up some trellis for flowering vines to break up the monotonous expanse. It might even be possible—with the neighbour's cooperation—to create a *trompe l'oeil*, a French expression meaning "an illusion of distance," or literally, "fool the eye." Usually this is achieved by trelliswork, mirrors, or murals mounted or painted onto a flat surface with an exaggeration of perspective to make the flat wall seem as though it is receding.

Another ruse to consider is a fake façade, such as an entranceway or a Greek temple. Columns that stand out in relief only a few inches from the flat wall and doors and windows that do not open—but merely serve as embellishment—can make unsightly walls more pleasant to look at.

Espaliered trees and shrubs are also excellent devices to camouflage monotonous expanses of masonry and concrete. Where sunlight is adequate, orchard fruits such as apples, pears, figs, and peaches should be considered. In shady areas camellias, climbing hydrangeas, English ivy, Southern magnolia, and firethorn can be used.

Generally, a necessary storage facility is a compost pile—a place to dump garden and kitchen waste which will rot down and provide valuable humus for enriching garden soil. Most tidy gardens have a space at the side of the property where the waste material is tipped into bins—usually three are needed: one with finished compost, one in the process of being filled, and a separate bin for decomposing leaves to make leaf mould, which generally takes longer to decompose and is especially valuable for bulb plantings, vegetables, and

Flowering vines trained over the roof of a garage help to make an attractive planting out of what might otherwise be an eyesore.

Pink doors effectively hide a space for storing rubbish bins.

PLANTS TO ESPALIER

Apples
(Prunus cultivars)
Yellow and red fruits are decorative

Camellia
(Camellia japonica)
Superb flowers in early spring

English Ivy
(Hedera helix)
Good for hard to plant places

Figs
(Ficus carica)
Delicious fruit, large leaves

Firethorn
(Pyracantha coccinea)
Beautiful red berries in autumn

Holly, English
(Ilex aquifolium)
Glossy leaves, red berries

Peaches
(Prunus cultivars)
Delicious fruits are decorative

Pears
(Pyrus cultivars)
Delicious fruits. Tolerates some shade

Southern Magnolia
(Magnolis grandiflora)
Massive white flowers, glossy leaves

Yew
(Taxus baccata)
Suitable for shaded locations

acid-loving plants like azaleas. The bins are generally square, made from treated wooden slats, up to shoulder height. Cylindrical compost bins made from metal and plastic are also available. They rest on a ventilated platform that helps provide air circulation.

However, compost can be made quite tidily without the need to box it in. A neat pile shaped like a Toblerone chocolate bar can be made by adding compost in layers—a mixture of equal parts green material (grass clippings, hedge prunings, fresh weeds) and dead material (sawdust, wood chips, dried stalks)—to speed the decomposition process.

The next most important utility area is a toolshed, which can also do double duty as a potting shed if it is constructed with that purpose in mind. A toolshed can serve as a beautiful architectural structure in the garden, in a rustic design or disguised as a pavillion, cottage, summerhouse, or small barn. To serve as a potting shed it needs work benches and windows to admit plenty of natural light. Toolsheds and potting sheds are frequently attached to a freestanding greenhouse for convenience.

Attached to a toolshed can be a simple shelter for the purpose of storing firewood. Usually this is little more than a wooden frame with a shingle roof. It's also a good policy to locate a cold frame—a low enclosure covered with glass to harden-off plants prior to transplanting in spring and to grow salad greens out of season—close to a toolshed. Using an east- or south-facing wall as the back wall of the cold frame is most effective.

Many people also like to include animal shelters as part of the garden landscape. A chicken house with a run, rabbit hutches, a dovecote, and a stable for a pony or pet pig are examples of animal shelters that can be decorative.

Places to store refuse containers should not only be screened from public view by a section of rustic fence or an evergreen hedge, but the dustbins should have frames to hold them upright so that if stray dogs or foxes try to raid them, they do not tip over.

If an area is needed to hang washing (many rural families like to air-dry certain clothing even when they have a washer and dryer), then a special enclosed courtyard can be constructed from inexpensive fencing, with a clothes reel rather than a long clothesline to hang clothes from.

This imaginative house sign is outside a house on a country road.

A tidy compost pile becomes a decorative feature in a vegetable garden. The garden waste is simply left to decompose and then spread over adjacent areas of the garden in spring.

A metal frame makes a good place to store firewood close to the house.

Butted against a toolshed, an attractive cold frame is used to grow lettuce out of season and to harden-off seedlings before transplanting.

135

AFTERWORD

Claude Monet's "Grande Allée."

Garden features are more than mere embellishments for an uninspired landscape. Whether artificial structures or natural highlights for decorative or practical purposes, their design and placement in the landscape can be crucial to a garden's aesthetic success.

Plantsmen know what plants will grow in a particular situation and how to care for them; architects know how the lines of a particular structure should look; but it is the artist in us that puts them together in a pleasing composition, enriching the landscape with colour, texture, and form.

Englishman Robin Loder, owner of Leonardslee Garden, in the south of England, alluded to the significance of garden focal points when defending his decision to cut down some grand old trees that were blocking a vista with a free-form lake in the distance as a focal point. As he explained it, "A view is worth a thousand blooms; a lake is worth ten thousand."

J. Drayton Hastie, owner of Magnolia Gardens, near Charleston, South Carolina (U.S.A.), also understands the value of garden highlights. Each year he tries to add at least one garden structure and one new major planting. He values the structures because they are permanent features that provide perpetual beauty; the plant accents he chooses with an inclination towards masses of colour because in such a large garden small plantings tend to get lost. In recent years he has concentrated on plants that provide good winter interest from berries, bark or winter silhouettes in order to provide colour through all four seasons.

Hiroshi Makita, an American landscape architect who designs Japanese gardens that have been acclaimed works of art, strongly advocates the use of garden features to achieve garden artistry—particularly through artificial structures. Features used in his gardens include free-form garden benches, low footbridges, high-arched rainbow bridges, and boats moored in lotus pools. Mr. Makita says that, "To me a garden is incomplete without some sign of human presence. All beautiful gardens represent control over nature—a taming of the wilderness—and the maintenance of a garden requires careful and constant attention to prevent nature reclaiming it as wilderness. A good man-made structure, properly placed in the landscape, framed by appropriate natural elements, signifies that gardens are not the design of nature, but the will of humans."

Nowhere is Mr. Makita's statement more evident than in Victoria, British Columbia (Canada), the location of beautiful Butchart Gardens. Here is the most intensively planted garden in North America. Not only is the garden a spectacular composition of strong garden features, it has turned an exploited landscape into a paradise, for most of the garden lies within an abandoned quarry where backhoe and bulldozer once ravaged the earth and left it denuded. In 1904 Jenny Butchart, the wife of the quarry owner, saw the empty pit as a fine place to start a garden with a treasury of garden features including Japanese and Italian gardens, majestic fountains, meandering paths, free-form lawns and raised flower beds with quarry stones for edging.

Indeed, gardens are the product of creative minds and proper use of garden features is a means to achieving excellence and inspiration in garden design.

SOURCES

The following list of specialists supply garden features either by mail-order or through dealerships.
Information or catalogues are available on request.

GARDEN FURNITURE

ARTISAN
Caxton Way, Thetford
Norfolk 1P24 3RY
*The Eden Collection of Scandinavian
beechwood furniture with white
lacquer or pink glaze finish. Dining
tables and chairs, armchairs,
sunloungers, and canopied sofas on
wheels.*

BARLOW TYRIE
Braintree
Essex CM7 7RN
Teak garden furniture.

BARRETTS OF EALING
Pitshangar Lane
Ealing, London W5
*Branson African Iroko furniture and
Gartub wooden tubs.*

THE CHELSEA GARDENER
125 Sydney Street
Kings Road, London SW3
*Furniture designed by David Mlinaric
and John Stefanidis. Also pergolas,
trellises, ornaments, and urns.*

CLASSIC GARDEN FURNITURE, LTD.
Audley Avenue
Newport, Shropshire TF10 7DS
Garden furniture of all kinds.

ANDREW CRACE DESIGNS
Bourne Lane
Much Hadham, Herts SG 10 6ER
*Iroko curved seats and benches. Also
gazebos and plant pots.*

GARDEN CRAFTS
158 New Kings Road
Fulham, London SW6 4LZ
*Traditional garden furniture, gazebos,
ornaments, statues, and troughs.*

GLOSTER LEISURE FURNITURE LTD.
Universal House
Pennywell Road
FREEPOST BS 2061
Bristol BS5 OYZ
*Solid teak furniture, also carving and
engraving services.*

GREEN BROS.
Dept. HO
Freepost 95
Hailsham, East Sussex BN27 1BR
*Lister Teak furniture. The Cirrus
collection of furniture and benches,
inspired by Chippendale and Lutyens.*

MARSTON AND LANGINGER
20 Bristol Gardens
Little Venice, London W9 2JQ
*Garden furniture including willow
chairs and loungers. Also cast iron
tables and chairs, and garden urns.*

NATIONAL TRUST WOOD FURNITURE
Joiners Shop
The National Trust
Erddig, Wrexham, Clwyd
Wales LL13 OYT
*Wooden garden furniture based upon
traditional designs.*

SUMMIT FURNITURE
Studio 11
318 Wandsworth Bridge Road
London SW6
Teak garden furniture.

VUOKKO SHOP
20 Morningside Road
Edinburgh EH10 4DA, Scotland
*Light, modern steel-framed benches
and tables.*

CONSERVATORIES AND GAZEBOS

AMDEGA
Dept. HG01/6
Faverdale
Darlington
Co. Durham DL3 OPW
*Luxury Victorian-style conservatories
in red cedar.*

ALEXANDER BARTHOLOMEW
277 Putney Bridge Road
London SW15 2PT
*Specialists in double-glazed
conservatories.*

JONATHAN GALE
72 Chatham Road
London SW11
*Individually designed Japanese-style
tea houses for the garden.*

MACHIN DESIGNS
Ransomes Dock
Parkgate Road
London SW11 4NP
*Curved roof conservatories built from
aluminium, glass, and stainless steel,
or with a wooden frame.*

OLLERTON ENGINEERING
Samlesbury Bottoms
Preston, Lancs. PR5 ORN
*Galvanized steel gazebos and rose
arches.*

TOWN AND COUNTRY
CONSERVATORIES
53 Ellington Street
Islington, London N7 8PN
*Fine glass buildings, individually
designed and built.*

TRELLISES, GATES, FENCES, AND STAIRWAYS

ALBION DESIGNS OF LONDON
12 Flitcroft Street
London WC2H 8DJ
Cast iron spiral staircases.

CLASSIC GARDEN FURNITURE, LTD.
Audley Avenue
Newport, Shropshire TF10 7DS
*Spiral staircases. Also a complete
range of garden furniture.*

COTTAGE CRAFT SPIRALS
Pear Tree Farm
Stubbings Lane
Chinley, Stockport
Cheshire SK12 6AE
Spiral staircases.

JACKSONS
118 Stowting Common
Nr. Ashford
Kent TN25 6BN
Wooden gates of all kinds.

RENZLAND FORGE
London Road
Copford, Colchester
Essex CO1 ILG
*Hand-built metal gates, railings, and
balustrading.*

TIGER DEVELOPMENTS LTD.
Deanland Road
Golden Cross
Nr. Hailsham, Sussex BN27 3RJ
*Wooden bridges for lakes, gardens,
and estates. Also gazebos.*

TRELLISWORKS LTD.
Clay Lane
Chichester
West Sussex PO19 3JG
Jointed trellis work and arches.

GARDEN ORNAMENTS AND SCULPTURES (INCLUDING POTS AND PLANTERS)

ARCHITECTURAL HERITAGE OF
CHELTENHAM
Boddington Manor
Boddington
Nr. Cheltenham, Gloucester GL51 OTJ
*Antique garden statuary and
ornaments in stone including seats,
tables, fountains, sundials, and
balustrades.*

C.H. BRANNAM LTD.
Litchdon Potteries
Barnstaple, Devon
Terra-cotta pots and urns.

THE CHELSEA GARDENER
125 Sloane Street
London SW3
*Terra-cotta pots and ornaments,
including amphorae.*

CHILSTONE
Sprivers
Horsmonden, Kent TN12 8DR
*Handmade stone garden ornaments,
fashioned according to antique
designs, including columns, coping,
balustrading, birdbaths, sundials,
statues, urns, obelisks, tables, seats,
and fountains.*

CLIFTON NURSERIES
CLIFTON Villas
Warwick Avenue
London W9
*Antique statuary, terra-cotta pots,
urns, columns, and figurines. Also
ornamental ironwork and other
garden accessories.*

CROWTHER OF SYON LODGE LTD.
Syon Lodge, London Road
Isleworth, Middlesex TW7 5BH (England)
*Antique garden ornaments, many
collected from famous old English
estates.*

HADDONSTONE
The Forge House
East Haddon
Northampton NN6 8DB
*Garden stone ornaments, urns, pots,
and jardinieres, handmade according
to 18th century designs.*

LANDSCAPE ORNAMENT COMPANY
Voysey House
Barley Mow Passage
Chiswick, London W4 4PN
*Statues, ornaments, and furniture from
reconstituted stone, bronze, timber,
and clayware materials.*

OLIVE TREE TRADING
Twickenham Trading Estate
Rugby Road
Twickenham, Middlesex TW1 1DG
*Terra-cotta pots, urns, columns, and
fugurines.*

MALCOLM POLLARD
42 East Park Parade
Northampton NN1 4LA
Garden sculpture.

SNAPDRAGON
Brian Hamilton
268 Lee High Road
London SE13
Chinese earthenware pots.

SOLSTICE
Unit E2 Colchester Factory Estate
Colchester Avenue
Cardiff CF3 7AP
Sundials.

WELFORD WEATHERVANES AND
SUNDIALS
23 Quiveysheys
Welford on Avon
Warwicks CV37 8PU
*Elegant and unusual sundials and
weathervanes.*

PAVING AND TILES

BORDERSTONE
Middleton Quarry
Middleton, Welshpool
Powys SY21 8DJ, Wales
*Pebbles and chips for borders and
paths.*

BRADSTONE GARDEN PRODUCTS
ECC Quarries Ltd.
Okus, Swindon, Wilts SN1 4JJ
*Paving (Octavian, Corinium, Sets, and
Riven) and Walling (Traditional,
Hadrian, Cotswall, and Aztec).*

BULMER BRICK AND TILE COMPANY
The Brickfields
Bulmer, nr. Sudbury, Essex C10 7EF
Handmade bricks and tiles.

J. DELVAUX AND CO.
Eastrea Road
Whittlesey, Peterborough, PE7 2AG
*Manufacturers of over six thousand
handmade components including
paving tiles, step units, fence posts,
modules, spiral staircases, and piping.*

RYE TILES
Ceramic Consultants
The Old Brewery
Wishward, Rye, Sussex TN31 7DH
Ceramic tiles.

THE TILE CENTRE
161-7 Borough High Street
London SE1 1HU
*Wall and floor exterior tiles. Also
ceramic tiles for swimming pools.*

TILES . . .
Dumfries Place
Newport, Gwent, Wales NT9 1YA
Marble wall and floor tiles.

WATER GARDENS

ANGLO AQUARIUM PLANT COMPANY
LTD.
Wayside, Cattlegate Road
Enfield, Middlesex EN2 9DP
Garden pools, fountains, plants, and fish.

INTERNATIONAL AQUATIC CENTRE
126/7 West Bar
Sheffield, South Yorks S3 APN

LOTUS WATERGARDEN PRODUCTS
260-300 Berkhamsted Road
Chesham, Bucks HP5 3EY

THE HANNAH PESCHAR SCULPTURE
GALLERY
Black and White Cottage
Standen Lane
Ockley, Surrey
Water sculptures.

STAPELEY WATER GARDENS
Dept. HG5
Stapeley, Nantwich, Cheshire
CW5 7LH
*Complete range of pond equipment
and aquatic plants.*

SURBITON AQUARIA COMPANY LTD.
Brighton Road
Surbiton, Surrey KT6 5LR

LIGHTING

ARTEMIDE GB
17-19 Neal Street
Covent Garden
London WC2H 9PU
*A selective range of modern Italian
designs in metal for patios, pools, and
conservatories.*

PETER BURIAN ASSOCIATES
Hillview
Vale of Health
London NW3
Waterproof lighting and lights for tubs.

JOHN CULLENS LIGHTING DESIGN
1 Woodfall Court, Smith Street
Chelsea, London SW3 4EJ

DEBONAIRE LIGHTING
Unit 6, Sparkbrook Street
Coventry, West Midlands
Victorian-style lamposts and lanterns.

HOZELOCK LTD.
Haddenham
Aylesbury, Bucks HP17 8JD
*Garden lighting. Also submersible
water pumps.*

J.H. MAY CASTINGS
15-20 The Oval
Hackney Road
Bethnal Green, London E2 9DX
Victorian-style London lamp posts.

JOHN O'SHEA EXTERIOR-LITE SERVICE
LTD.
Unit 4, The Empire Centre
Imperial Way, Watford WD2 4YH
*Full range of Bega Lighting, including
underwater lighting, wall bracket
lighting, underlighting, and
spotlighting for trees and plants.*

CHRISTOPHER WRAY'S LIGHTING
EMPORIUM
600 Kings Road
Chelsea, London SW6 2DX
*Victorian-style street lamps and
accessories, coach lamps, Tiffany
lights, decorative lighting for
conservatories, and clip lights for
exterior use.*

INDEX

BIBLIOGRAPHY

Brookes, John. *The Small Garden.* New York: Macmillan, 1978.

Beckett, Carr & Stevens. *The Contained Garden.* London: Frances Lincoln, 1986.

Chamberlin and Pollock. *Fences, Gates & Walls.* Tucson, AZ: HP Books, 1985.

Chamberlin, S. *Hedges, Screens & Espaliers.* Tucson, AZ: HP Books, 1983.

Church, Thomas D. *Gardens Are For People.* New York: McGraw Hill, 1983.

Cowell, F.R. *The Garden as a Fine Art.* New York: Houghton Mifflin, 1978.

Crow, Sylvia. *Garden Design.* New York: Hearthside Press, 1983.

Douglas, Frey, Johnson, Littlefield, Van Valkenburgh. *Garden Design.* New York: Simon & Schuster, 1984.

Engel, David. *Japanese Gardens For Today.* Rutland, VT: Charles Tuttle, 1959.

Fleming and Gore. *The English Garden.* London: Michael Joseph, 1979.

Gothein, Marie-Louise. *A History of Garden Art.* New York: Hacker Art Books, 1979.

Hayakawa, Masao. *The Garden Art of Japan.* New York: John Weatherill, 1973.

Johnson, Hugh. *The Principles of Gardening.* New York: Simon & Schuster, 1983.

Keswick, Maggie. *The Chinese Garden.* New York: Rizzoli, 1978.

Landis and Moholt. *Patios & Decks.* Tucson, AZ: HP Books, 1984.

Lees, Carlton B. *Gardens, Plants & Man.* Englewood Cliffs, NJ: Prentice Hall, 1970.

MacCaskey, Mike. *Lawns & Groundcovers.* Tucson, AZ: HP Books, 1982.

Morris, Edwin T. *The Gardens of China.* New York: Charles Scribners, 1982.

Page, Russell. *The Education of A Gardener.* New York: Random House, 1983.

Rose, James. *Creative Gardens.* New York: Rheinhold, 1958.

Saito Katsuo. *Magic of Trees & Stones.* New York: Japan Publications, 1965.

Shephard, Paul. *Man in the Landscape.* New York: Alfred A. Knopf, 1967.

Weber, Nelva M. *How to Plan Your Own Home Landscape.* New York: Bobbs-Merrill, 1976.

Wilkinson and Henderson. *House of Boughs.* New York: Viking, 1985.

ABOUT THE AUTHOR

Derek Fell, writer and photographer, specializes in photographing gardens worldwide, with an emphasis on garden design. He lived 25 years in England before moving to the United States to become a naturalized American citizen. In addition to travelling widely throughout North America, he has visited gardens throughout Europe, Africa and the Orient.

A frequent contributor to *Architectural Digest, The New York Times Magazine, Connoisseur, Americana, Woman's Day* and *Garden Design,* Fell is winner of more awards from the Garden Writers Association of America than any other garden writer, including Best Book, Best Magazine Article, and Best Photography.

Presently, Fell is creating a beautiful new "water garden" on his property in Bucks County, Pennsylvania. Featuring a pond with spillway, it also includes three styles of bridges, terraces with a fountain and urns, boulders, a boat dock, arbours, benches and colourful plantings of water-lilies, water iris, ostrich ferns and candelabra primulas. Further afield, Fell designed the Bamboo Lake and its moon bridge at Magnolia Plantation, South Carolina (U.S.A.), and worked as a consultant on garden design to The White House during the Ford Administration.